I0462085

Learn Kubernetes

Container orchestration using Docker

Arnaud Weil

Learn Kubernetes

Container orchestration using Docker

Arnaud Weil

ISBN 978-0-244-25802-3

To my parents, for teaching me freedom and making sure I can enjoy it.

To my wonderful family. Your love and support fueled this book.

To my readers who suggested improvements to this book, especially Doğan Kartaltepe for your ongoing and dedicated support.

Contents

CONTENTS

Introduction

What this book is not

I made my best to keep this book small, so that you can learn Kubernetes quickly without getting lost in petty details. If you are looking for a reference book where you'll find answers to all the questions you may have within the next 4 years of your Kubernetes practice, you'll find other heavy books for that.

My purpose is to swiftly provide you with the tools you need to create and run your first cloud-ready application using Kubernetes, then be able to look for more by yourself when needed. While some authors seem to pride themselves in having the thickest book, in this series I'm glad I achieved the thinnest possible book for my purpose. Though I tried my best to keep all of what seems necessary, based on my 16 years experience of teaching.

Prerequisites

This book is for anyone who needs to run software on Kubernetes. Whether you're a developer, a DevOps manager or a technician, this book should help you plan and run Kubernetes workloads.

I assume that you have no previous knowledge about containers or containers orchestration.

How to read this book

This book's aim is to make you productive as quickly as possible. For this we'll use some theory, several demonstrations, plus exercises. Exercises appear like the following:

 Do it yourself: Time to grab your keyboard and code away to meet the given objectives.

In code samples, a backslash is used in order to wrap long lines. Do not type theses backslashes when you copy code from the book.

Tools you need

The only tools you'll need to work through this book are the following:

- A Windows, Linux or Mac machine that meets the specifications for Docker Desktop or Minikube, or the ability to create a PaaS cluster (Azure AKS, Google GKE, Amazon EKS).
- A text editor.

Source code

All of the source code for the demos and do-it-yourself solutions is available at https://bitbucket.org/epobb/ kubernetesbookfiles

It can be downloaded as a ZIP file[1], or if you installed GIT you can simply type:

```
git clone https://bitbucket.org/epobb/kubernetesbookfil\
es.git
```

---

[1] https://bitbucket.org/epobb/kubernetesbookfiles/downloads

1. Why Kubernetes

1.1 DevOps challenges

Opposing Devs and Ops

In the DevOps trend, the Dev and Ops teams have conflicting goals:

Dev team seeks	Ops team seeks
Frequent deployments and updates	Stability of production apps
Easy creation of new resources	Manage infrastructure, not applications
	Monitoring and control

As an agile developer I want to frequently publish my applications so that deployment becomes a routine. The rationale behind this is that this agility makes the "go to production" event a normal, frequent, completely mastered event instead of a dreaded disaster that may awake monsters who will hit me one week later. On the other hand, it is the Ops team that will have to face the user if anything goes wrong in deployment - so they naturally want stability.

Conflicts with dependencies

A typical web application looks something like the following:

The application is made of files served by an HTTP server (Apache here, but it could be Kestrel, IIS, NGINX, ...), a runtime (PHP 5.6 here) and a development framework (Wordpress 4.9 here).

The dependencies and files are all placed together on a server. Since managing those dependencies is time-consuming, similar apps are typically grouped on the same server, sharing their dependencies:

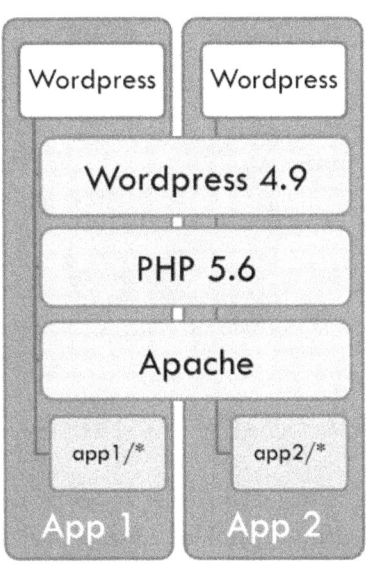

Now suppose you want to upgrade the PHP runtime from version 5.6 to 7.2. But the version change induces breaking changes in the applications that hence need to be updated. You need to update both *App 1* and *App 2* when proceeding with the upgrade. On a server that may host many apps of this type, this is going to be a daunting task and you'll need to delay the upgrade until all apps are ready.

Another similar problem is when you want to host say *App 3* on the same server, but *App 3* uses the Node.JS runtime together with a package that when installed changes a dependency that is used by the PHP runtime. Conflicts between runtimes are not scarce, so you probably faced that problem already.

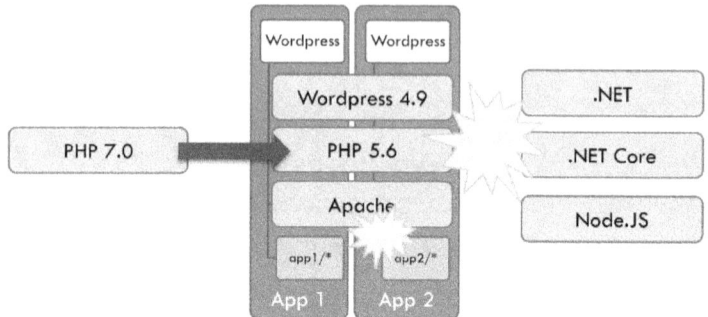

High availability and updates

When a server application needs to provide high availability, the solution is well-known: place a reverse proxy in front of it, and duplicate the server as many times as needed. In case one server crashes, users will be routed to another server. In our previous Wordpress application example, this means duplicating the server together with all of its dependencies:

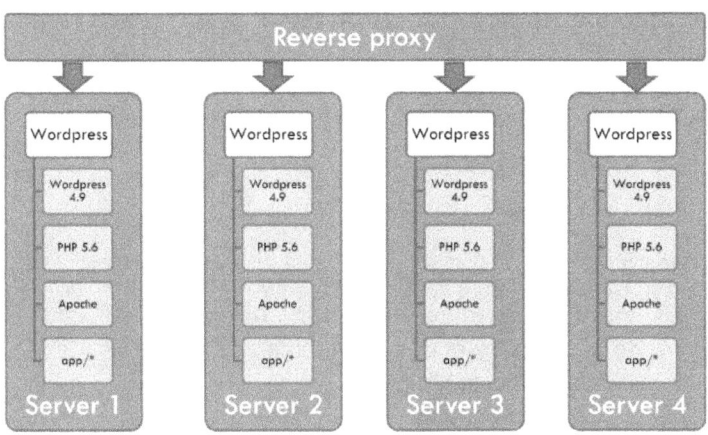

That is only going to make things worse when upgrading: we'll need to upgrade each server's dependencies, together with all of the conflicts that this may induce:

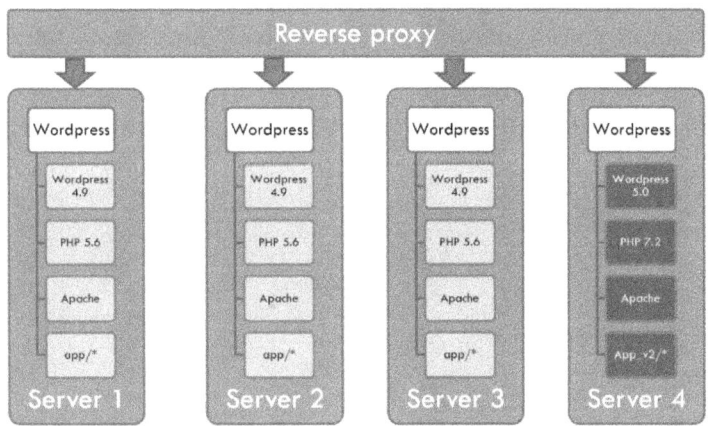

Of course, in such a case the update process will depend on the application and its dependencies. Don't even try to tell your admins about DevOps if you want to remain alive.

1.2 Containers

> This chapter and the following ones are a short introduction to containers and Docker. If you want to learn more about those concepts, you can read my Learn Docker[a] book.
>
> ---
> [a]https://leanpub.com/dock

International commerce faced the same delivery problem: we are trying to deliver software as fluently as possible, and commerce needs to deliver goods as fluently as possible.

In the old times, it took days to load a ship with goods:

Classic ship loading

The ship remained docked at the pier during a few days while each good was being loaded into it. Goods had varying sizes and handling precautions, and ships had storage of varying types and sizes. That's what made loading (and unloading) a slow process. Slow and costly: it required many people to do it, plus the immobilization of the ship and goods has a cost.

A solution was found: containers. The idea is very simple: use boxes of a standard size, and fill them with whatever you want. You now only need to handle standardized boxes no matter what they contain. Problem solved: the ship can be tailored to host many containers in a way that allow for fast (un)loading thanks to standardized tools like cranes:

Container ship loading

In fact, the whole transport chain (trains, trucks) can be tailored to manage containers efficiently:

Freight train

Believe it or not: Docker containers are very similar. When you create an image, you stuff your software into a container image. When a machine runs it, a container is created from the image. Container images and containers can be managed in a standardized way, which allows for standard solutions during a containerized software's lifecycle:

- common build chain;
- common image storage;
- common way to deploy and scale up;
- common hosting of running containers;
- common control and monitoring of running containers;
- common ways to update running containers to a new version.

The most important part being: whatever the real software inside the container (.NET Core, PHP, Node.JS, Ruby, Java, Python, Go, …), it can be handled in a common way. Isn't that a DevOps' dream?

Containers run in a reproducible way whether they run on Linux, Azure, a public cloud or your private cloud. That makes them great choice in a cloud-first strategy. For instance, do you remember the last time you installed and ran a reverse proxy or HTTP server? Here's how you run one with Docker:

```
> docker run -p 8085:80 nginx
```

Now I can just point my browser to http://localhost:8085 and I can see that NGINX is running. Mind you, the same command could deploy any web application.

Applications running inside of containers are not only shipped easily, they run isolated from each other. Your typical server would look like:

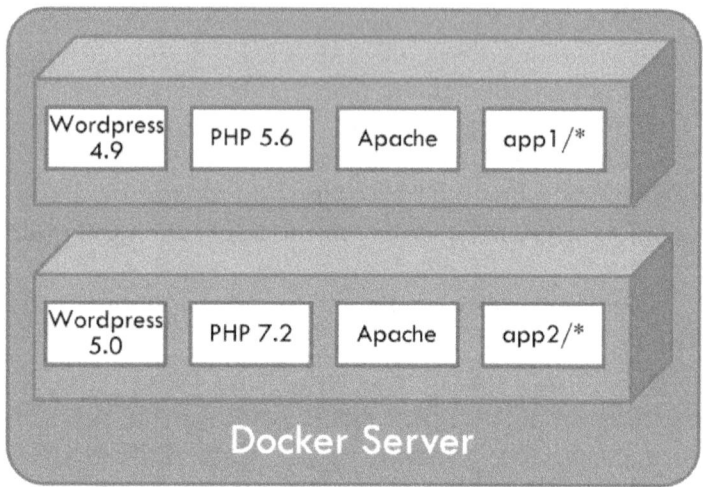

Each container encapsulates its own dependencies. Which means you can migrate the PHP runtime from version 5.6 to 7.2 in a container without affecting other. Any other container that would use, e.g., Node.JS would not interfere with any of the Wordpress containers.

In short, containers could be described as lightweight virtualization: they offer isolation and reproducibility just like virtualization, but they consume much less resources than traditional virtualization.

1.3 Docker containers

Docker is available on many platforms: Linux, Windows, Mac and public cloud providers.

There are three concepts I need you to grasp so that we can begin smoothly: **containers**, **images** and **registries**.

A *container* is what we eventually want to run and host in Docker. You can think of it as an isolated machine. Or a virtual machine if you prefer.

From a conceptual point of view, a *container* runs inside the Docker host isolated from the other containers and even the host OS. It cannot see the other containers, physical storage, or get incoming connections unless you explicitly state that it can. It contains everything it needs to run: OS, packages, runtimes, files, environment variables, standard input and output.

Any container that runs is created from an *image*. An image describes everything that is needed to create a container: it is a template for containers. You may create as many containers as needed from a single image.

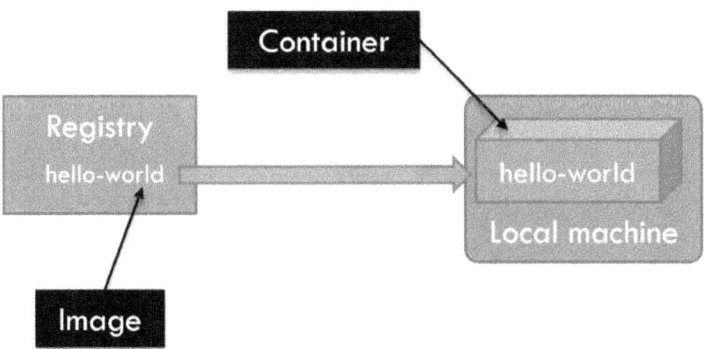

Images are stored in a *registry*. Think of the registry as a server that hold the images you want to deploy to any server.

> Although you can read the rest of that book without knowing how an image is built, I'll go quickly over it for those interested.

A Docker image is created using the *docker build* command and a *Dockerfile* file. The *Dockerfile* file contains instructions that state how the image should be built.

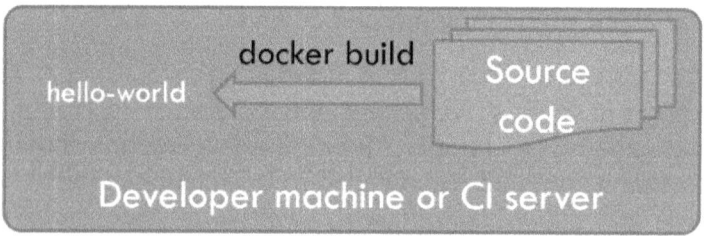

Here is an example Dockerfile file:

```
FROM wordpress:4.9.4-php5.6-apache
COPY ./sources /var/www/html
```

As you can see, it is a plain text file. The first instruction, FROM, states the name of the image from upon which ours is built. Then come instructions that state what is added to that base image. Here we copy files from the *sources* folder (that is located in the same place as the Dockerfile) and place them inside the */var/www/html* folder of the image.

In order to actually create the image, we simply run the following command:

```
> docker build -t my-wordpress:1.0 .
```

1.4 Deploying images

A Docker Registry is basically an image store that offers the following functions:

- ability to store various images;
- ability to store various tags for the same image;
- an HTTP API that allows to push images from a machine that produces them, or pull images to a machine that runs containers from those images;
- TLS-secured connection to the API in order to avoid man-in-the-middle attacks.

There are many registries available. You can use the publicly available Docker Hub or use a private registry of your own.

Whatever the Registry you choose, publishing an image is a three-step process:

1. build your image (*docker build*) with the appropriate prefix name or tag (*docker tag*) an existing one appropriately;

2. log into the Registry (*docker login*);
3. push the image into the Registry (*docker push*).

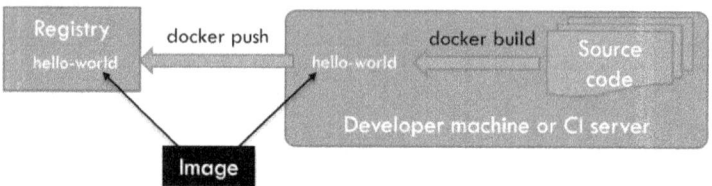

1.5 The need for container orchestration

When you highly rely on containers and/or have high workloads, managing containers will raise several concerns. Think about how you would:

- Deploy and maintain applications that use many containers.
- Deploy and maintain applications that spawn containers over different machines.
- Manage resources used by the containers.
- Scale applications up and down by adding and removing containers, possibly across different machines or dynamically provisioned ones.
- Update your applications.
- Update the servers running your applications without application outages.

- Switch from one host to another.

Such problems are elegantly solved by container orchestration systems. Kubernetes is such a container orchestration platform. You can think of it as an operating system for containers. It automates deployment, scaling, and operation of containerized applications across a cluster of host machines.

1.6 What's K8s?

K8s is simply an abbreviation for Kubernetes. Take the letters between the leading "K" and trailing "s", count them, and replace them with that count. Since "ubernete" is 8-letters long, it can be replaced with an "8", which gives us K8s.

While we're at it, there's a complete Kubernetes glossary[1] on the Kubernetes site.

---

[1] https://kubernetes.io/docs/concepts/overview/what-is-kubernetes/

2. Kubernetes cluster

2.1 Parts of a Kubernetes cluster

A Kubernetes cluster's goal in life is to run your containers. It will stubbornly make sure your containers are running. Here's a schema of your containers running:

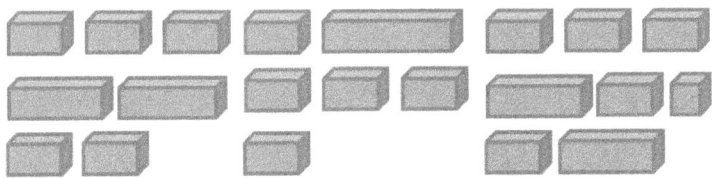

Life would be too simple if everyone understood what we do as a living, so most people tend to use complicated words. You probably already heard about **pods**, and you may even wonder what are the differences between a pod and a container.

Let's make it simple: you can consider for now that a pod is a container.

A pod is actually much more than a single container, but until we explain the difference you're actually safe considering that a pod is a container.

As such, a Kubernetes cluster's goal in life is to run your

pods. In order to do so, it uses actual machines (they can be physical or virtual machines) called **nodes**.

Here's a Kubernetes cluster running your pods on its nodes:

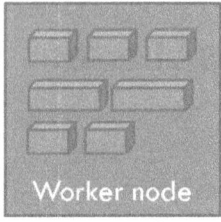 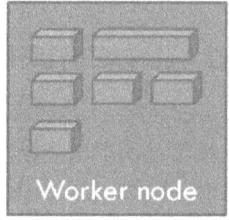 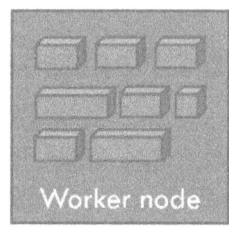

Pods are the actual pieces of software you want to run, and nodes are the hardware pieces that run them. Think of nodes as a resource that can run your pods. Pods require CPU and memory, nodes provide this CPU and memory. The fact that nodes are part of a Kubernetes cluster allow them to be spread over the cluster so that we can get many benefits like resilience, high availability and horizontal scaling.

There are two types of nodes: worker nodes and master nodes. The schema we just saw pictures only **worker nodes** because those are the nodes that actually run your pods. **Master nodes** don't run your pods: they control the worker nodes in order to make sure that they respect your will. We saw that a Kubernetes cluster's goal in life is to run your pods, and the master nodes are those who make this happen.

Here's our cluster, now with the master nodes included:

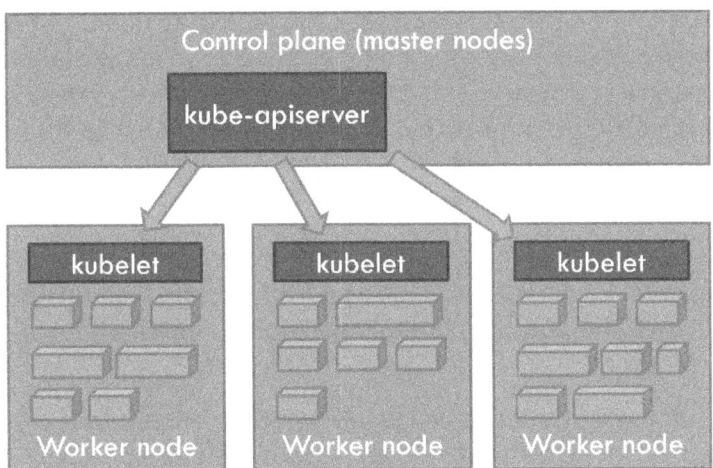

Master nodes are to worker nodes what managers are to technicians in real life: their work is to make sure that others do the visible work. Much like developers write the actual software while their managers distribute the software pieces to be written over the available developers, worker nodes run the actual user-facing software (pods) while their master nodes distribute the pods to be run over available worker nodes.

There can be a single master node, but there are usually several of them in order to achieve high availability. Whether there is one or several master nodes, they are logically grouped together into what we call the **control plane**.

Worker nodes are non-critical resources. In case one of them goes away, the control plane will start new pods on the remaining nodes in order to replace those that were running on the missing node. You'll have to find out how many worker nodes your cluster needs: too many of them means that you won't use each to its fullest capacity, but too little means that you may not be able to afford losing some of them. Hopefully nodes can be added and removed dynamically.

The control plane receives your orders through its API server. Each worker node runs a kubelet daemon that allows the control plane to manage its pods and other resources.

Since your Kubernetes cluster wants to ensure that your pods run as desired, it uses a few more components:

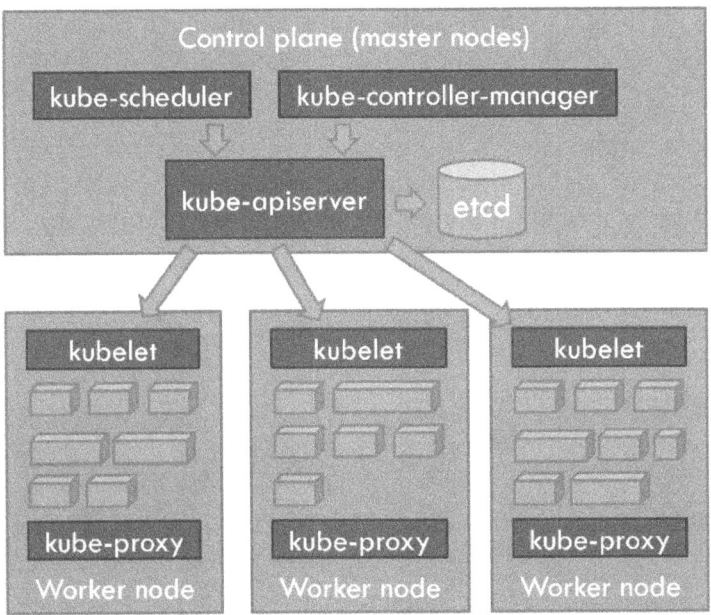

You don't need to understand those extra components in order to make your first steps in Kubernetes, so the previous schema would be a good simplified reference. However, please allow me to introduce you to the hidden workers that will make our Kubernetes cluster stronger.

etcd is a database that stores the desired state of your cluster so that the control plane can take appropriate actions on the worker nodes in order to reach and keep that state no matter what happens. And many things may happen inside your cluster: a worker node may become unavailable or a new one can join the cluster, a pod can die or need to be updated or scaled out. Thanks to the etcd database the control plane can ensure it has a reference of what state needs to be reached. As long as half of the master nodes are available, etcd works correctly.

kube-scheduler is responsible for creating pods on the right nodes, and **kube-controller-manager** makes sure that the required number of pods are running in an expected state.

Now that we saw the big picture, we can go back to a simpler representation of your Kubernetes cluster:

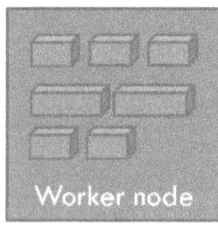 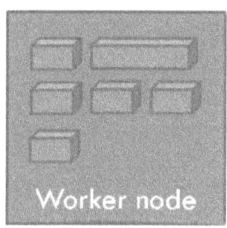 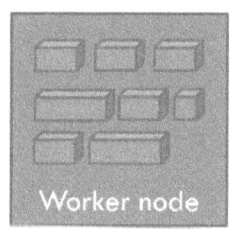

As we run our applications on the cluster day to day, what matters is that Kubernetes offers a worker / pod abstraction: pods are the units of your software that can be ran atomically, and worker nodes are the units of hardware that offer the CPU and memory resources needed for that. Your software requires CPU and memory, which Kubernetes allocates on all of the available worker nodes.

2.2 Creating a cluster

There are several ways to get a running Kubernetes cluster, and what you choose depends on what you want to do with it. Choices fall within 3 categories:

Type	Setup	Scales out
Development workstation	Easy	No
Cloud PaaS	Easy	Yes
Private	Complex	Yes

What we want now is to have a working Kubernetes so that we can learn how to use Kubernetes and prepare our workloads for a production cluster, so the "development workstation" solutions are those we'll head for. In order to run user-facing applications though, we'll need a private or Cloud Pass Kubernetes cluster. Let's review those.

Development workstation

Before you send your application to a distant production cluster, you'd rather set it up and test it on a Kubernetes cluster on your machine, and that's one reason why you need a local Kubernetes cluster on your development machine. Other reasons are exactly the same that make you install a local setup for any development platform instead of using a distant one.

Luckily, setting up a Kubernetes cluster on your machine is an easy task in most cases. There are at least two options: Docker Desktop and Minikube. Both set up a single-node Kubernetes cluster.

Docker Desktop includes Docker development tools plus a Kubernetes cluster out of the box. If you are going to run Docker containers in your cluster, that's a good candidate especially on Windows and Mac machines.

Minikube is more flexible. It lets you decide which Kubernetes version you want to use, which extensions are installed, which container runtime will be needed. Flexibility comes at a price so be prepared to spend some time setting it up, but on Linux machines it's quite straightforward.

Cloud PaaS

For your production workloads, you can get Kubernetes clusters from major cloud providers. A basic setup of these usually is a mundane task, and activities like upgrading or securing your cluster are mostly effortless or automated.

Another advantage of using a PaaS Kubernetes cluster is that you can add or remove nodes as necessary, since you are running on a Cloud infrastructure. Since Kubernetes is a perfect choice for running resource-intensive workloads thanks to its scaling capabilities, having the ability to add virtual machines with virtually no limit is definitely a plus for those of you who will face high or varying workloads. For that matter, many PaaS cloud offerings allow you to have dynamic nodes provisioning:

they can start or stop virtual machines when your cluster reaches peak usage.

Some Cloud Kubernetes offerings are:

- Azure AKS: you are only charged for worker nodes. You don't need to manage the master nodes and you don't pay for them. AKS enables automatic provisioning of worker nodes when your cluster reaches peak usage.
- Google GKE: you are only charged for worker nodes, and it enables automatic provisioning of worker nodes when your cluster reaches peak usage.
- Amazon EKS, RedHat OpenShift, IBM CKS, Heptio Kubernetes Subscription.

Private

Some use cases cannot be covered by a Cloud Kubernetes offering. For instance, a client of mine needs to create and manage Kubernetes clusters at designated data centers that are airtight secured. kubeadm is part of the Kubernetes distribution. It helps setting up and maintaining a Kubernetes cluster using basic commands like init, join, upgrade and reset.

Since kubeadm is composable, there are several tools that build upon it and help you with setting up a Kubernetes cluster in various contexts. For instance, you can use:

- Kubespray in order to setup custom clusters both

whether in the Cloud or on bare metal. It can use Ansible or Vagrant.
* Kops in order to setup custom clusters at some Cloud providers like AWS and GCE.

Such tools can enable you to get a running cluster in matter of hours. However, be aware that correctly securing a cluster requires some efforts, and maintaining a cluster does need time and dedication. It's not just about backing up or upgrading your servers: business needs that lead to using Kubernetes often imply high availability, automatic scaling and reliability, which in turn imply work for those administering the cluster.

In case you build your own cluster, make sur that you can provide:

* High availability of the control plane
* Extensibility and automatic repair of worker nodes
* Security (first of which is securing communication between nodes and to etcd)
* Upgrades
* etcd backup and restore
* Volumes backup and restore

2.3 Exercise - Set up your development cluster

 Objective: get a working development cluster.

You need to create a Kubernetes cluster that you will use for this book's exercises. Select one of the following options:

- Install Docker Desktop[1]
- Install Minikube[2]
- Create a PaaS cluster in the Cloud.

Once you are done, you should be able to run the following command successfully:

```
kubectl get nodes
```

2.4 Exercise solution

This exercise doesn't have detailed guidance since your experience may vary according to many factors, and installation details are provided on the respective tools' pages.

2.5 Connecting to a cluster

The kubectl tool

Once your Kubernetes cluster is ready, you need a tool in order to interact with it. kubectl is a command-line

---

[1] https://www.docker.com/products/docker-desktop
[2] https://kubernetes.io/docs/tasks/tools/install-minikube/

tool that meets most needs. It is flexible and complete enough to be used during development deployments as well as from your continuous-delivery server (you sure use a CI/CD chain, don't you?). It works in connection with your local development cluster as well as with productions clusters. This is where it fits:

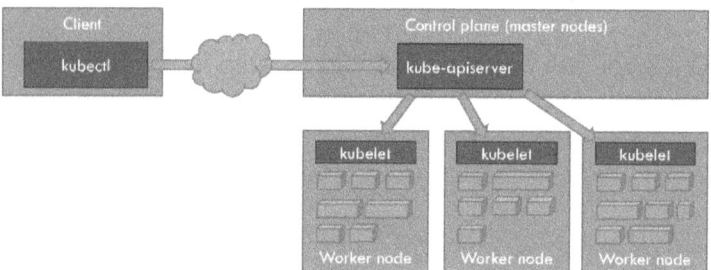

The kubectl tool sends commands to your Kubernetes cluster through the cluster API. It allows for cluster inspection and monitoring (listing nodes, pods, and other cluster resources), and enables for creation, deletion and update of elements inside your Kubernetes cluster.

You can get kubectl from there[3]. Make sure that the kubectl version fits the Kubernetes cluster version of the cluster you want to target. In order to check that everything is fine, you can run the following command:

```
kubectl version
```

If everything is set up correctly, you should get an output similar to the following:

---

[3]https://kubernetes.io/docs/tasks/tools/install-kubectl

```
Client Version: version.Info{Major:"1", Minor: ... }
Server Version: version.Info{Major:"1", Minor: ... }
```

The *Client* part shows what you have on your machine, and the *Server* part shows information about the Kubernetes cluster. But wait, which cluster? And what if nothing appears in the *Server* part on your machine?

Kubectl contexts

The `kubectl` tool connects to a Kubernetes cluster thanks to a **context**. Each context stores credentials for a given user in a given cluster.

Having several contexts is an obvious way to connect to different clusters (development and production clusters for instance), but it also is an handy way to connect to the same cluster using different credentials. For instance it allows you to test that the credentials used by a CI/CD tool work correctly.

You can list the current contexts using the `get-contexts` command:

```
> kubectl config get-contexts
```

```
CURRENT    NAME
           some-cluster
           anotherOne
*          docker-desktop
           cloudk8s
```

Note the star to the left of "my-cluster". It indicates that this is the current cluster. In other words, any command issued using the `kubectl` tool will act on that cluster.

In order to use another context, you can use the following command:

```
kubectl config use-context <context-name>
```

> In case you installed Docker Desktop, it enables you to list and switch contexts using a right-click on it system tray icon.

Oftentimes the tools you will use to connect to clusters you create will create a new context entry for you, but you may add entries using the `set-cluster`, `set-credentials` and `set-context` subcommands of the `kubectl config` command.

Basic commands

From there, we can use some kubectl commands:

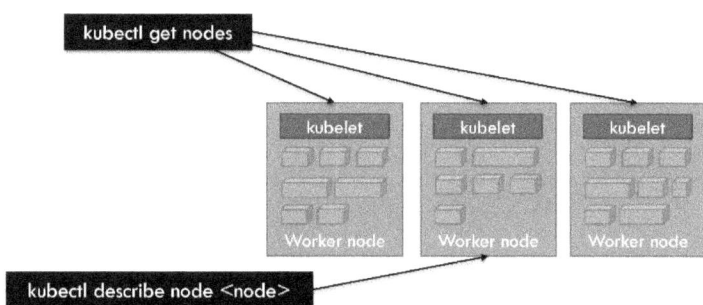

The get nodes command lists the master and worker nodes of your cluster. The get node command will describe an individual node; you need to provide it with a node name that you got from the get nodes command.

```
> kubectl get nodes
NAME            STATUS  ROLES   AGE     VERSION
aks-1923416-1   Ready   agent   27d19h  v1.14.6
aks-1923416-2   Ready   agent   27d19h  v1.14.6

> kubectl describe node aks-1923416-1

Name:    aks-1923416-1
Roles:   agent
(lots of information about that node)
```

In some environments like Azure AKS, master nodes are managed for you and won't get listed by a `get nodes` command. The sample above shows such an case.

3. Tooling

There are many tools aimed at making your Kubernetes life easier. Since Kubernetes can fully be API-driven, you could even write your own. However, for most needs you should need only two : a text editor and kubectl.

Since we already saw kubectl, let me introduce some optional tools that may help you through your Kubernetes path.

3.1 Kubernetes Dashboard

Though kubectl is an extremely powerful swiss-knife tool for Kubernetes, those who aren't used to command-line interfaces often turn to me with an anxious face asking whether there is a graphical tool. Yes, there is, and it's the Kubernetes Dashboard. Not an essential tool, but one that may reassure those used to graphical user interfaces instead of command-line tools.

The Dashboard is a web interface which may be accessed using a browser. It allows for simple cluster supervision in a user-friendly interface. It also allows for basic creation of pods and services.

Its home page provides you with a high-level view of your cluster's workloads:

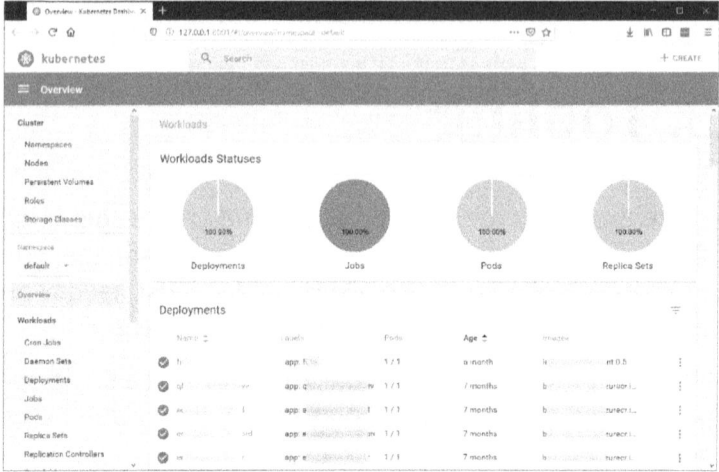

It allows you to dig into Kubernetes objects including the nodes. For instance, here's the page showing details of a worker node:

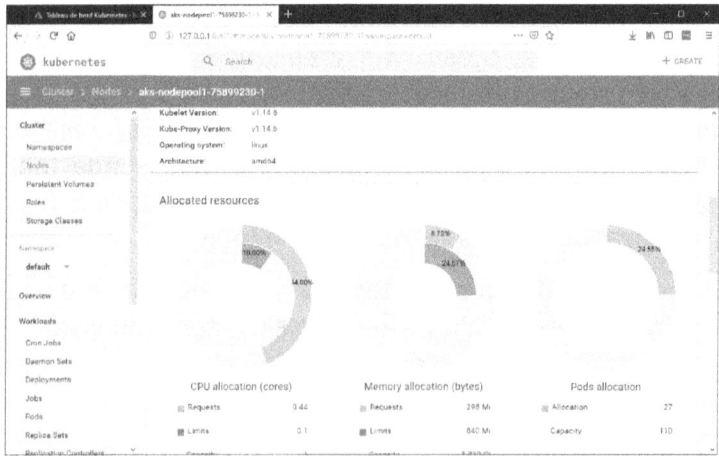

You may notice a "create" button located in the upper right. When clicked, a page that allows for creating a Deployment and an optional Service appears:

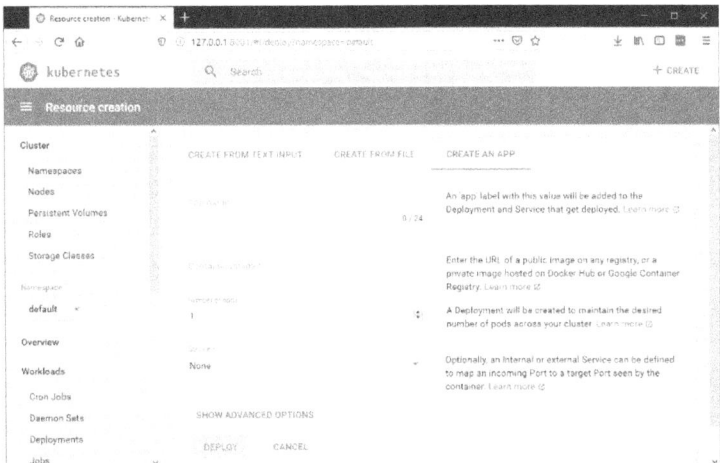

The Dashboard may be installed following the instructions on the project page[1]

For those running on Azure AKS, there should be a link to the Dashboard on the details page of your cluster. When running an RBAC-enabled AKS cluster, it may be necessary to create the appropriate rights for the Dashboard to access you cluster's details:

---

[1] https://github.com/kubernetes/dashboard/

```
kubectl create clusterrolebinding kubernetes-dashboard \
--clusterrole=cluster-admin --serviceaccount=kube-syste\
m:kubernetes-dashboard
```

3.2 Visual Studio Code

Routine work with a Kubernetes cluster involves manip-
ulating YAML files, which are text files. This needs a good
text editor. In case you don't have one already, I can only
recommend Visual Studio Code[2] since it is lightweight,
flexible and cross-platform.

Visual Studio Code is customized through the use of extensions. Click on the "Extensions" button in the toolbar
(located to the left). There's a *Kubernetes* extension from
Microsoft (ms-kubernetes-tools.vscode-kubernetes-tools)
that provides a GUI for mundane Kubernetes and Helm
(see later) tasks. It's like a mix between the Kubernetes
Dashboard and kubectl and I can only recommend it.
Here's the extension in action:

---
[2]https://code.visualstudio.com/

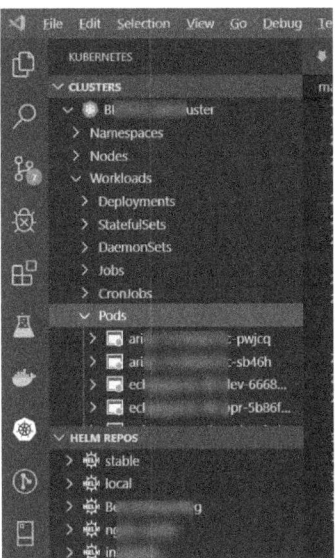

3.3 Helm

In a later chapter we'll learn about Helm and how to create *charts* that can be deployed using Helm. It's a common deployment tool in the Kubernetes world since it takes Kubernetes deployments one step further. Per se, Kubernetes deployments are easy and great in comparison to what someone could achieve without it, but Helm makes the following actions easy:

- vary deployments according to parameters
- deploy several resources as one single entity
- rollback the deployment

It's not yet time to create our Helm *charts*, but we'll need to use Helm in order to deploy an *Ingress controller* and then to create our charts so let me introduce it. Basically, Helm is installed both on your deployment machine (your machine or CD server) and in the Kubernetes cluster. The component installed inside the cluster is called *Tiller*. Tiller tracks the deployments made and takes care of upgrading or rolling them back when required to do so. From a conceptual standpoint a Helm installation looks like this:

In order to avoid loosing time later, now is a right time to install Helm in case it isn't. Just follow those steps.

Run the following command:

```
helm version
```

In case Helm is already installed you get something along those lines:

```
Client: &version.Version{SemVer:"v2.12.3", ...}
Server: &version.Version{SemVer:"v2.12.3", ...}
```

In that case, you can skip to the next chapter. Otherwise, follow on.

In case it is missing on the client side (your machine), you need to get the *helm* executable and add it to your path. It can be done manually or through a package manager, instructions are available at https://github.com/helm/helm#install.

 The following instruction is for an unsecured install. Make sure you secure it further.

Install the Tiller part of Helm on the server using the following command:

```
helm init --history-max 200
```

4. Running pods

4.1 Deployments and ReplicaSets

As we saw, a Kubernetes cluster is a set of available CPU and memory resources that will run your Pods. Pods should be considered as ephemeral since many things can cause their death: they may crash, may need to be killed because they consume too much resources, they may need to be replaced by a newer version during application upgrades, and they may disappear simply because the node that runs them is powered off or becomes unavailable in some other way.

Fear not: Kubernetes will make its best to have your Pods run whatever the circumstances. This means restarting as many of them as needed, on available worker nodes. The way it does this is through a *ReplicaSet* object. A ReplicaSet ensures that a required number of Pods are running in a sane state, starting new ones or stopping unnecessary or insane ones as needed.

In order to manage version changes, which mean reducing Pods in the older ReplicaSet and growing them in the newer ReplicaSet, Kubernetes uses a *Deployment* object. Here's how it all looks:

That may look complicated, but it's actually simple if you consider all of its responsibilities. For most of your work, you can think of it in a simple (less accurate) way:

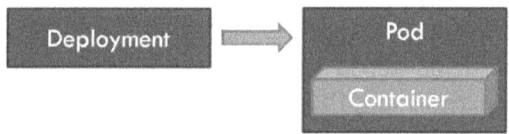

We'll come back to ReplicaSets later when detailing upgrade strategies, but for now just consider that you create Deployments in order to run and upgrade your Pods.

How do you create a Deployment ? There are actually two ways to do so: imperative and declarative. Imperative looks easy so we'll begin with them. Declarative looks more complex, but in the long run it will make your work much easier.

4.2 Imperative commands

The `kubectl create` command allows you to imperatively create a Kubernetes resource. Here's how you would create a Deployment of the *hello-world* Docker image:

```
> kubectl create deployment hello --image=hello-world

deployment.apps/hello created
```

We can then check that the Deployment was actually created:

```
> kubectl get deployments -l app=hello

NAME    READY   UP-TO-DATE   AVAILABLE   AGE
hello   0/1     1            0           1m45s
```

There are several things worth noting here: the status of the Deployment, and the selector. Let me explain both.

The selector *-lapp=hello* is optional. It means "return only those that have a label named *app* whose value is *hello*". If your cluster is empty you could as well not use that selector. Labels are metadata you can place on Kubernetes objects. Selectors don't change how an object behaves; they allow you to select similar objects later on.

The status reported above looks quite strange because it states that 0 of 1 expected resource is available, though one is up to date. This is simply due to the fact that the *hello-world* image is a short-running image that outputs some text and stops, hence the Pod is short-lived. Had we launched a long-running image like an HTTP server, it would still be available.

In details, the columns returned by the *kubectl get deployment* command have the following meaning:

- NAME: this is the name of the Deployment. We provided it in the *kubectl get deployment* command.
- READY: this is the number of up and running Pods created by this Deployment versus the ones we requested. We didn't specify any quantity of Pods so the default is 1. 0 means that there is no running Pod, and this is due to the fact that the Pod was short-lived and stop.
- UP-TO-DATE: this is the number of Pods that could actually run the requested *hello-world* image. This means the image could successfully be pulled from a Docker registry.
- AVAILABLE: this is the number of Pods available to your users. Again, the fact that a 0 is reported here is due to the fact that we ran a short-lived image.

In fact, things are a little more complicated. Remember that a Deployment's aim is to ensure that your Pod is running whatever happens ? That means that once our short-lived Pod stops, the deployment creates a new one. So if you run the above *kubectl get* command several times in a row you will see that at some points in time there is one Pod marked as "Ready". Mind you, Deployments are not for short-lived Pods and we should have used a Job instead so that the Pods is not restarted uselessly. More about Jobs later, but an interesting feature is that between two Pod restarts the Deployment will wait during increasing times; which means that a malfunctioning Pod should not stop your cluster due to excessive restarts.

Let's now see the output generated by the Pod. It's the actual output of the *hello-world* image.

```
> kubectl logs -l app=hello
```

```
To try something more ambitious, you can run an Ubuntu \
container with:
 $ docker run -it ubuntu bash
```

```
Share images, automate workflows, and more with a free \
Docker ID:
 https://hub.docker.com/
```

```
For more examples and ideas, visit:
 https://docs.docker.com/get-started/
```

The output was truncated to the last 10 lines. We could add the *–tail* switch in order to output more, like:

```
> kubectl logs -l app=hello --tail 100
```

Now let's look at the Pod itself. The *kubectl get* command accepts names of many other Kubernetes resource types, hence we can use it for Pods:

```
> kubectl get pods -l app=hello
```

```
NAME       READY  STATUS          RESTARTS  AGE
hello-f8   0/1    CrashLoopBackOff  32        22m
```

We can see some details about the Pod, which reveal the reason why the it isn't running: *CrashLoopBackOff* means that it's in a waiting state because of a crash inside the Pod.

We could dig further into the Pod for details, but that's enough for now. Let's get back to our interactive command. The problem with an interactive command is that its outcome depends on the current state of resources inside the cluster. If I run the initial command again, it has a different output:

```
> kubectl create deployment hello --image=hello-world

Error from server (AlreadyExists): deployments.apps "he\
llo" already exists
```

As you can see, the command fails because a Deployment with the same name was already created. Should you manage a cluster manually, you can check whether the Deployment already exists and use different commands according to the current Deployment state. But who wants to manually manage applications inside a Kubernetes cluster in the long run?

Obviously, we want to be able to automate creation and update of resources inside our Kubernetes cluster. We could write scripts that take into account the current state of resources before deciding what to do, but this is going to be tricky to test and complicated to write and maintain. Since the advantage of imperative commands is their simplicity, once we get into tricky things we can consider using a more simple tool. Good news: declarative commands will make automation much simpler.

Before we move on to declarative command, let's clean the resources we created. In fact, we just need to delete the Deployment, which in turn will delete the Pod it created (and the ReplicaSet).

```
> kubectl delete deployment hello

deployment.extensions "hello" deleted
```

> Caution: when naming Kubernetes objects (everywhere a *name* is required), make sure you only use lowercase letters and/or dashes, and a maximum of 64 characters.

4.3 Exercise - Use imperative commands

 Objective: get acquainted with creating a resource imperatively.

The *learnbook/k8s-pinger:0.6* image pings *www.google.com* every 5 seconds.

Create a Deployment named *pinger* that deploys the *learnbook/k8s-pinger:0.6* image.

Display the Pods and check that there is one running the *learnbook/k8s-pinger:0.6* image.

Display the *pinger* Pod logs in order to confirm that it is actually pinging the remote server.

4.4 Exercise solution

- Open a command-line.
- Run the following command:

```
kubectl create deployment pinger --image=learnbook/k8s-\
pinger
```

- Make sure that the output states that the Deploy-ment was created.
- Run the following commands:

```
kubectl get pods -l app=pinger
kubectl logs -l app=pinger
```

You should get an output similar to the following one:

```
NAME          READY   STATUS     RESTARTS   AGE
pinger-7489   1/1     Running    0          32s

round-trip min/avg/max = 12.100/12.100/12.100 ms
Sleeping for 5 seconds

Pinging at: ...
PING www.google.com (216.58.209.228): 56 data bytes

--- www.google.com ping statistics ---
1 packets transmitted, 1 packets received, 0% packet lo\
ss
round-trip min/avg/max = 9.735/9.735/9.735 ms
Sleeping for 5 seconds
```

4.5 Exercise - Observe Kubernetes handle a failing pod

 Objective: check what happens when a Pod fails.

Display Pods and Deployments. Check that there is one instance of the *pinger* Pod available.

Delete the pinger Pod (the Pod, not the Deployment) using the following command:

```
kubectl delete pod -l app=pinger
```

Display Pods and Deployments. Check that the previous Pod is being shut down and that a new Pod was started in order to replace it.

Delete the *pinger* Deployment. Display Pods and Deployments. Check that all *pinger* Pods are deleted.

4.6 Exercise solution

- Open a command-line.
- Run the following commands:

```
kubectl get deployments
kubectl get pods
```

Note that a single instance of the *pinger* Pod is available:

```
> kubectl get deployments
NAME      READY   UP-TO-DATE   AVAILABLE   AGE
pinger    1/1     1            1           15m

> kubectl get pods

NAME             READY   STATUS    RESTARTS   AGE
pinger-7489665   1/1     Running   0          15m
```

- Run the following commands:

```
kubectl delete pod -l app=pinger
kubectl get deployments
kubectl get pods
```

Note the new Pod that was created to replace the one that is being deleted. This is due to the fact that the Deployment is still there, making sure that a Pod keeps running.

- Run the following commands:

```
kubectl delete deployment pinger
kubectl get deployments
kubectl get pods
```

Note that the Deployment and accompanying Pods were deleted or are in the process of being deleted.

4.7 Declarative commands

There's a better way to manage Kubernetes objects on the long run: declarative commands. Instead of telling Kubernetes *what to do*, you tell Kubernetes *what you expect*. This allows Kubernetes to reach the expected state no matter what the initial state is. Which in turn simplifies your deployment and maintenance routines.

For instance, suppose you tell Kubernetes that you want two Pods. The actions it will take will depend on the actual state of the Kubernetes cluster at the moment you provide your command and later on:

- If the cluster has no Pod, it will create two.
- If the cluster has one such Pod, it will create another one.
- If the cluster has 4 such Pods, it will delete two.
- If the cluster has two such Pods running an older version of the image, they will be replaced by new ones.
- If a cluster Node crashes that was running any of those two Pods, the corresponding number of Pods will be created on another Node.

There's one drawback to declarative commands: they look more complex than imperative commands at first. This is due to the fact that they are verbose because they describe all the values of the expected state that are not default ones. But you'll get used to it on the long run, plus it's good practice anyway to make things explicit.

Declarative commands bring many advantages:

- Simpler than imperative commands for application maintenance.
- Easily used in a CI/CD chain.
- Apply good practices like: Infrastructure as Code and Single Source of Truth.

Given an imperative command, Kubernetes takes the appropriate steps for reaching the expected state described by the command.

Running declarative commands

In order to run declarative commands, the commonly used way is to create a YAML file that describes the expected state and provide that file to the *kubectl apply* command.

Here's an example YAML file (more about that syntax later):

deploy.yaml

```
apiVersion: apps/v1beta1
kind: Deployment
metadata:
  name: my-front
spec:
  replicas: 1
  template:
    spec:
      containers:
        - name: my-front
          image: my-wordpress:1.0
          ports:
            - containerPort: 80
```

And here's the command to make the Kubernetes cluster conform to that description:

```
> kubectl apply -f deploy.yaml
```

After running that command, Kubernetes creates a Deployment, which in turn creates a ReplicaSet, which creates a Pod running a container from the *my-wordpress:1.0* image:

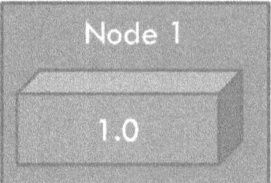

A state to be reached

Kubernetes will try to reach the state described in the YAML file whatever the starting state of the cluster. That makes it very handy to deploy an application equally on a local machine, a test cluster or a production one: it will mostly be a matter of providing the same YAML (and varying parameters or environment variables, more about that later).

It also means that scaling out or upgrading a Kubernetes application - a task that may have been daunting for non-containerized applications - becomes a simple one: all you need to do is apply the desired YAML file.

For instance, let's scale out our application. Scaling out means that we create more Pods in order to handle more workload : if one Pod on a Node can handle a given amount of users, four Pods on several Nodes will handle a higher number. Another advantage of scaling out is that your application becomes more resilient: losing one Pod out of four is no big deal, at least much less that losing your only Pod.

So, let's scale out. It's a simple matter of changing one number in the YAML file and use the same *kubectl apply* command as before.

deploy.yaml

```
apiVersion: apps/v1beta1
kind: Deployment
metadata:
  name: my-front
spec:
  replicas: 4
  template:
    spec:
      containers:
        - name: my-front
          image: my-wordpress:1.0
          ports:
            - containerPort: 80
```

```
> kubectl apply -f deploy.yaml
```

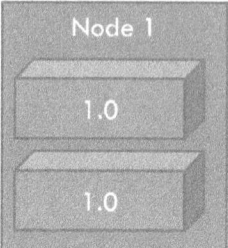 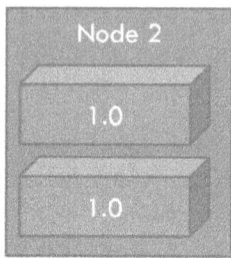

Kubernetes will compare the submitted file and the current cluster state. Since there is already one running Pod, it is going to create 3 other Pods running the same image. Easy and smooth. Downscaling would be just as easy: I can change the *replicas* count to a lower number and Kubernetes will terminate the Pods that are not needed anymore.

Kubernetes creates the new Pods in a deliciously clever way: in runs one more Pod, and checks that the Pod actually works; in case the Pod works, it proceeds with the next Pod. That way, it avoids filling a cluster with invalid Pods. And this is just the default behavior, which can be configured.

How would we upgrade those 4 running Pods to a newer version of the image? Just as easily: we change the *image* part of the YAML file and run the same *kubectl apply* command.

deploy.yaml

```
apiVersion: apps/v1beta1
kind: Deployment
metadata:
  name: my-front
spec:
  replicas: 4
  template:
    spec:
      containers:
      - name: my-front
        image: my-wordpress:1.1
        ports:
        - containerPort: 80
```

```
> kubectl apply -f deploy.yaml
```

Since there are 4 running Pods of version 1.0 in my cluster, they need to be replaced with Pods from version 1.1. Kubernetes will create one new 1.1 Pod, and wait to check if the Pod works. In case the Pod doesn't work, Kubernetes stops creating 1.1 Pods and version 1.0 remains available. In case the Pod works, Kubernetes deletes one 1.0 Pod and proceeds with a second 1.1 Pod, and so on.

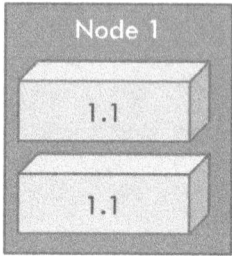 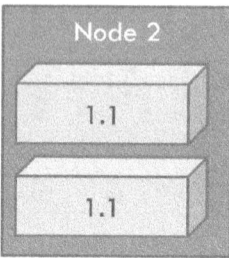

In short, your application remains stable during updates and doesn't eat up more resources that it ought to; and the best part is that all of this is automated by default.

Again, the declarative commands work whatever the starting state. If you *kubectl apply* the previous YAML to an empty cluster, it will just create the 4 Pods one by one. This is a very convenient feature, because applications are generally deployed more often to a development cluster than to a production one. You could define your CI/CD chain to publish to a development cluster each time code is pushed, and to a test cluster only when a tag is added to the repository or some other manual action is taken; that would be done very easily, using exactly the same YAML file and same *kubectl apply* except that it would be done more often on the development cluster than on the test one.

Should you want to use a single Kubernetes cluster in order to deploy both a development and a test version of your application, this is also easy: Namespaces can isolate your Kubernetes objects from one another. We'll learn about Namespaces later on.

Declarative syntax

Let's have a closer look at the YAML file we just applied to the Kubernetes cluster, and how you can get help writing it.

The `kubectl` command can also output the necessary YAML so that when you create a declarative YAML file you start from an existing file instead of a blank page. All you have to to is add the `--dry-run` and `-o yaml` switches to an imperative command.

For instance, the same *kubectl create deployment* command I used earlier would output the following YAML when we add the necessary switches:

```
> kubectl create deployment hello  image=hello-world -\
-dry-run -o yaml

apiVersion: apps/v1
kind: Deployment
metadata:
  creationTimestamp: null
  labels:
    app: hello
  name: hello
spec:
```

```
replicas: 1
selector:
  matchLabels:
    app: hello
strategy: {}
template:
  metadata:
    creationTimestamp: null
    labels:
      app: hello
  spec:
    containers:
    - image: hello-world
      name: hello-world
      resources: {}
status: {}
```

That YAML is more verbose than what I used for my
demos because it includes default values. That's a good
thing since we want this as a base template. Another
point worth noting is that the actual YAML will vary
according to the version of the Kubernetes cluster you
run it against: it is generated using the Kubernetes API,
and that API varies slightly from one Kubernetes version
to another.

If you prefer JSON you can also use it. Both YAML and
JSON are formats for a textual representation of objects,
lists of objects, and object properties. I use YAML in this
book since this is the format most seen for Kubernetes
declarative commands. The YAML specification is avail-

able on the official site[1] and you can get a quick startup from the preview[2] section of the site or that quickstart[3].

There are four main properties in the document used to create a deployment (the one that we just obtained from the *kubectl* command, or the ones we used earlier in the book):

- apiVersion: states the Kubernetes API version that the following properties use.
- kind: the Kubernetes object we are creating or updating. Here, a *Deployment*.
- metadata: data that should be attached to the Kubernetes object. It's used for finding Kubernetes objects for several purposes. We used it earlier when creating a selector to see logs (remember `kubectl logs -l app=hello`), and it will also be used for Kubernetes objects to reference one another.
- spec: describes what the Deployment should be like:
  - template: describes what the Pods managed by this Deployment should be like.
  - replicas: number of Pods that this Deployment should have. This involves creating Pods when this number is increased or a Pod dies, or deleting Pods when this number is decreased or that they exist with a different template.
  - strategy: states how the Deployment should proceed with the current Pods in case a pre-

---

[1] https://yaml.org/
[2] https://yaml.org/spec/1.2/spec.html#Preview
[3] https://rollout.io/blog/yaml-tutorial-everything-you-need-get-started/

vious version of this Deployment should be updated; we'll see more about that in the Update
strategies chapter.

Declarative commands

Let's recapitulate how a Kubernetes cluster is managed
with declarative commands.

This is how you create objects:

```
> kubectl apply -f deploy.yaml
```

This is how you update objects (same command as
above):

```
> kubectl apply -f deploy.yaml
```

And this is how you completely delete objects:

```
> kubectl delete -f deploy.yaml
```

While Kubernetes can be quite complex, the simplicity
of these commands blatantly illustrates how complex
operations are made simple by Kubernetes.

In all of the above commands, you can replace the file
name with a folder name. In that case, all of the files
in the folder will be passed through the command. This
enables you to write each Kubernetes object in a separate
file instead of packing them all together.

For instance, consider the following file (truncated for brevity):

deploy.yaml

```
apiVersion: apps/v1beta1
kind: Deployment
 . . .
 - - -
apiVersion: v1
kind: Service
 . . .
```

> The --- separator allows for several objects to be described in a single YAML file.

It would be applied with the command:

```
> kubectl apply -f deploy.yaml
```

You could instead replace it with two files in a *k8s* folder:

k8s/deployment.yaml

```
apiVersion: apps/v1beta1
kind: Deployment
 . . .
```

k8s/service.yaml

```
apiVersion: v1
kind: Service
. . .
```

And those files would be applied using a single command:

```
> kubectl apply -f ./k8s
```

4.8 Exercise - Create resources using declarative commands

 Objective: get acquainted with creating a resource declaratively.

In a YAML file, describe a Deployment named *pinger*
that deploys the *learnbook/k8s-pinger:0.6* image with an
app=pinger label.

Use the *kubectl apply* command to create the corresponding Deployment in the Kubernetes cluster.

Display the Pods and Deployments and check that the
Deployment and corresponding Pod were created.

4.9 Exercise solution

- Create a file named *pinger-deployment.yaml* with the following contents:

```
apiVersion: apps/v1beta1
kind: Deployment
metadata:
  name: pinger
spec:
  template:
    metadata:
      labels:
        app: pinger
    spec:
      containers:
      - name: pinger
        image: learnbook/k8s-pinger:0.6
```

- Open a command-line in the folder where you created the above file.
- Run the following commands:

```
kubectl apply -f pinger-deployment.yaml
kubectl get deployment
kubectl get pods
kubectl logs -lapp=pinger
```

You should get an output similar to the following one:

```
> kubectl apply -f pinger-deployment.yaml

deployment.apps/pinger created


> kubectl get deployment

NAME      READY   UP-TO-DATE   AVAILABLE   AGE
pinger    1/1     1            1           52s


> kubectl get pods

NAME          READY   STATUS    RESTARTS   AGE
pinger-646    1/1     Running   0          92s
```

```
> kubectl logs -lapp=pinger

round-trip min/avg/max = 12.100/12.100/12.100 ms
Sleeping for 5 seconds

Pinging at: ...
PING www.google.com (216.58.209.228): 56 data bytes

...
```

Environment variables

The containers that run in your Pods will often need to be provided environment variables. An environment variable can be read from the executable running inside the container; it's a common way to provide extra information like a the URL of an API or a connection string to a data store.

Environment variables may be provided to your Pods using the *env* property of the *container* definition. Here is an example definition of a container running with two environment variables:

```
apiVersion: apps/v1beta1
kind: Deployment
metadata:
  name: my-front
spec:
template:
    spec:
      containers:
      - name: my-front
        image: my-wordpress:1.0
        env:
        - name: someName
          value: "some value"
        - name: someOtherName
          value: "some other value"
```

When the executable running inside the *my-wordpress:1.0* image queries the value of the "someName" environment variable, it receives a value of "some value".

4.10 Exercise - Update a Pod created declaratively

 Objective: update a Pod that was created declaratively, providing environment variables to the container.

Update the YAML file that you created in the previous

exercise. You should pass the following environment variables to the container:

- target: www.qwant.com
- delay: 30

Since the container is running the *learnbook/k8s-pinger:0.6* image, those variables specify that the container should ping the www.qwant.com address every 30 seconds.

Display the Pods and Deployments and check that the Pod was updated.

Display the Pod logs selecting those with a *app=pinger* label. Check that pings are made to *www.qwant.com*.

At some point in the logs you can see that both *www.google.com* and *www.qwant.com* are pinged. Can you explain why?

4.11 Exercise solution

- Edit the file named *pinger-deployment.yaml* with the following contents:

```
apiVersion: apps/v1beta1
kind: Deployment
metadata:
  name: pinger
spec:
  template:
    metadata:
      labels:
        app: pinger
    spec:
      containers:
      - name: pinger
        image: learnbook/k8s-pinger:0.6
        env:
        - name: target
          value: "www.qwant.com"
        - name: delay
          value: "30"
```

- Open a command-line in the folder where you created the above file.
- Run the following commands:

```
kubectl apply -f pinger-deployment.yaml
kubectl get deployment
kubectl get pods
kubectl logs -lapp=pinger --tail 20
```

You should get an output similar to the following one:

```
> kubectl apply -f pinger-deployment.yaml

deployment.apps/pinger configured
```

Note the *configured* phrasing instead of the *created* one you had in the previous exercise. This is due to the fact the the Deployment already existed.

```
> kubectl get deployment

NAME     READY   UP-TO-DATE   AVAILABLE   AGE
pinger   1/1     1            1           3m54s

> kubectl get pods

NAME         READY   STATUS        RESTARTS   AGE
pinger-646   1/1     Terminating   0          62s
pinger-688   1/1     Running       0          8s
```

We can see that Kubernetes created a new Pod in order to run it with the appropriate environment variables. The previous Pod is terminated once the new one is up and running.

```
> kubectl logs -lapp=pinger --tail 20


round-trip min/avg/max = 11.246/11.246/11.246 ms
Sleeping for 5 seconds


Pinging at: ...
PING www.google.com (216.58.201.228): 56 data bytes


--- www.google.com ping statistics ---
1 packets transmitted, 1 packets received, 0% packet lo\
ss
round-trip min/avg/max = 11.083/11.083/11.083 ms
Sleeping for 5 seconds


Pinging at: ...
PING www.qwant.com (194.187.168.100): 56 data bytes


--- www.qwant.com ping statistics ---
1 packets transmitted, 0 packets received, 100% packet \
loss
Sleeping for 30 seconds
```

The log shows pings to both *www.google.com* and *www.qwant.com*
because it creates the new Pod then terminates the
previous one. There's a time during which both Pods are
alive, so the *kubectl logs* command will get the output
from both since we select using the label applied to the
Pods. If the command is ran later, once the first Pod
has completely stopped, the log will show only pings to
www.qwant.com.

Controllers

Creating a Deployment in order to manage your Pods allows you to ensure that there is always (more or less, depending on cluster conditions and updates) a given number of Pods running at any given time. There are other types of Pod controllers that you may want to create depending on your needs:

- ReplicaSet / Deployment: run Pods that should always be there.
- Job: run Pods in a fire-and-forget way : Kubernetes makes sure that a given number of Pods run to completion (that is, the main executable in the container terminates without an error).
- CronJob: same as a Job, but on a recurring basis. It's like creating a Job on a regular basis.
- DaemonSet: ensures that a Pod is running on each cluster Node. This is useful for Kubernetes-related Pods that should be present on every node like *kube-proxy*.

Job and CronJob are appropriate for containers with executables that stop after they have done their work. Kubernetes expects them to stop and will not restart them. Deployment, on the contrary, is appropriate for containers with executables that should not stop (for instance a web server) : Kubernetes restarts the Pod in case it stops (since that means there is an error).

4.12 Debugging

What can go wrong *will* go wrong, according to Murphy's law, so we'd better have tools to understand what goes wrong. Common errors on a Pod include:

- Container image that can't be found. For instance, when it wasn't published by a CI/CD yet or that you provided a wrong name.
- Error inside the container's main executable. That is, the executable returns with an error.

In both cases, the Kubernetes controller restarts the container. In order to ensure that system resources aren't starved by problematic Pods, a growing delay is introduced between two container restarts.

The first thing you can do is to get details about the problematic Pod. Run the following command:

```
kubectl describe pod <name>
```

This will allow you to see whether there was an image problem, or the state of the Pod otherwise. In case you have a problem with the executable inside the container, displaying logs should help:

```
kubectl logs -lapp=hello
```

Remember that logs are the actual output of the container, so what you get here depends on the verbosity of the container.

In case you need to run code inside the Kubernetes cluster in order to interact with a problematic Pod (for instance initiate network communications to it or check the Node's disk), you can actually run another debugger Pod inside the cluster:

```
kubectl run -i --tty busybox --image=busybox -- sh
```

The above command runs a container with the *busybox* image and keeps your terminal connected to it. This allows you to use the bunch of utilities packed inside the busybox image[4] in order to inspect the problematic Pod.

4.13 Exercise - Debugging failing Pods

 Objective: observe how Kubernetes handles errors and find the cause of an error.

Create a YAML file that describes a Deployment of the *learnbook/debugging1:0.6* image labelled with *app=debugging*.

---

[4]https://hub.docker.com/_/busybox

Use the *kubectl apply* command in order to create the corresponding Deployment in the Kubernetes cluster.

Display Pods and Deployments in order to make sure that the Deployment was created.

What is the state of that Deployment? What is the state of the corresponding Pod?

Use the *kubectl describe* command in order to understand what happened inside the Pod.

Create a YAML file that describes a Deployment of the *mongo-express:0.49.0* image labelled with *app=debugging2*. Use the *kubectl apply* command in order to create the corresponding Deployment in the Kubernetes cluster.

Display Pods and Deployments in order to make sure that the Deployment was created.

You can see that the corresponding Pod is restarted again and again. Explain why.

4.14 Exercise solution

- Create a file named *debugging1-deployment.yaml* with the following contents:

```
apiVersion: apps/v1beta1
kind: Deployment
metadata:
  name: debugging1
spec:
  template:
    metadata:
      labels:
        app: debugging1
    spec:
      containers:
      - name: debugging1
        image: learnbook/debugging1:0.6
```

- Open a command-line in the folder where you created the above file.
- Run the following commands:

```
kubectl apply -f debugging1-deployment.yaml
kubectl get deployment
kubectl get pods
# replace name with actual Pod name
kubectl describe pod debugging1-64f9ffd9bd-d7l6k
```

You should get an output similar to the following one:

```
> kubectl apply -f debugging1-deployment.yaml
```

```
deployment.apps/debugging1 created
```

```
> kubectl get deployment
```

```
NAME          READY    UP-TO-DATE    AVAILABLE    AGE
debugging1    0/1      1             0            24s
```

You can see that one Pod in the Deployment is up to date, but not ready.

```
> kubectl get pods
```

```
NAME             READY    STATUS               RESTARTS    AGE
debugging1-85    0/1      ImagePullBackOff     0           56s
```

You can see that the Pod is not ready, and its status is "ImagePullBackOff".

```
> kubectl describe pod debugging1-85994956bc-cnlnq
```

```
...
Containers:
  debugging1:
    Container ID:
    Image:            learnbook/debugging1:0.6
...
Events:
  Age                      Message
```

```
  - - - -                 - - - - - - -
. . .
  30s (x6 over 111s)  Back-off pulling image ...
  16s (x4 over 111s)  Pulling image "learnbook/debuggin\
g1:0.6"
  16s (x4 over 111s)  Failed to pull image ......
  16s (x4 over 111s)  Error: ErrImagePull
  3s (x7 over 111s)   Error: ImagePullBackOff
```

You can see the events that led to the ImagePullBackOff status: Kubernetes tried to pull the image (4 times over two minutes) but it couldn't.

Actually, this is due to the fact that the *learnbook/debugging1:0.6* image doesn't exist.

- Create a file named *debugging2-deployment.yaml* with the following contents:

```
apiVersion: apps/v1beta1
kind: Deployment
metadata:
  name: debugging2
spec:
  template:
    metadata:
      labels:
        app: debugging2
    spec:
      containers:
```

```
- name: debugging2
  image: mongo-express:0.49.0
```

- Open a command-line in the folder where you created the above file.
- Run the following commands:

```
kubectl apply -f debugging2-deployment.yaml
kubectl get deployment
kubectl get pods
kubectl logs -lapp=debugging2
```

You should get an output similar to the following one:

```
> kubectl apply -f debugging2-deployment.yaml

deployment.apps/debugging2 created


> kubectl get deployment

NAME          READY   UP-TO-DATE   AVAILABLE   AGE
debugging1    0/1     1            0           13m
debugging2    0/1     1            0           26s
```

You can see that one Pod in the Deployment is up to date, but not ready.

```
> kubectl get pods
```

```
NAME            READY   STATUS              RESTARTS   AGE
debugging1-85   0/1     ImagePullBackOff    0          13m
debugging2-7c   0/1     CrashLoopBackOff    1          31s
```

You can see that the Pod was restarted once and has a CrashLoopBackOff status. Kubernetes restarts the Pod because its main executable is crashing.

```
> kubectl logs -lapp=debugging2
```

```
. . .
    at Pool.emit (events.js:211:7)
    at Connection.<anonymous> (/node_modules/mongodb-co\
re/lib/connection/pool.js:270:12)
. . .
    at Connection.emit (events.js:214:7)
    at Socket.<anonymous> (/node_modules/mongodb-core/l\
ib/connection/connection.js:175:49)
. . .
```

You can see that the executable inside the Pod is a Node.JS application and that it sent its stack trace to the log (its output). In the trace, you can see that the failing code is related with a connection to MongoDB.

Actually, the *mongo-express:0.49.0* image expects an environment variable with the connection string to a MongoDB database, because it's a web front-end for

administering a database. That's why you get this message, because I didn't ask you to provide an environment
variable to the Pod.

4.15 Exercise - Delete created objects

 Objective: free up resources created in the
previous exercises.

Display the currently running Pods and Deployments.

Using the *kubect delete* command and the YAML files
created in the previous exercises, delete all of the Pods
and Deployments created in the previous exercises.

4.16 Exercise solution

- Open a command-line in the folder where you created the previous YAML files.
- Run the following commands:

```
kubectl get deployment
kubectl get pods
kubectl delete -f pinger-deployment.yaml
kubectl delete -f debugging1-deployment.yaml
kubectl delete -f debugging2-deployment.yaml
kubectl get deployment
kubectl get pods
```

You should get an output similar to the following one:

```
> kubectl get deployment

NAME          READY   UP-TO-DATE   AVAILABLE   AGE
debugging1    0/1     1            0           12h
debugging2    0/1     1            0           12h
pinger        1/1     1            1           31h


> kubectl get pods

NAME               READY   STATUS              RESTARTS   AGE
debugging1-85      0/1     ImagePullBackOff    0          12h
debugging2-7c      0/1     CrashLoopBackOff    8          12h
pinger-688bf5      1/1     Running             2          31h


> kubectl delete -f pinger-deployment.yaml

deployment.apps "pinger" deleted
```

```
> kubectl delete -f debugging1-deployment.yaml

deployment.apps "debugging1" deleted


> kubectl delete -f debugging2-deployment.yaml

deployment.apps "debugging2" deleted


> kubectl get deployment

No resources found.


> kubectl get pods

No resources found.
```

Is there always one container in a Pod?

Pods often run a single container but that isn't always
true. This is a point of detail, but a Pod may run several
containers. You mostly don't want to do that since Pods
are ephemeral resources, but it may be interesting in
cases like the one pictured below:

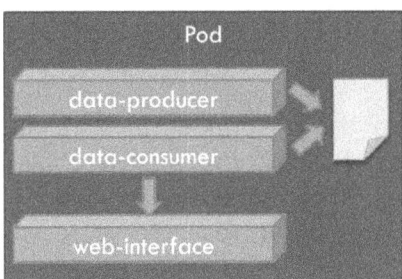

In that case, the *data-producer* container produces transient files that are read by the *data-consumer* container. The *data-consumer* container itself exposes an API to the *web-interface* container.

In that case, containers are grouped inside the same Pod because they are tightly bound together. While they could be ran in separate Pods, there would be some overhead in communicating between the containers across different Pods.

Note that there is a drawback: in case you want to scale out the corresponding application, you can only duplicate the whole Pod. In the case that the *web-interface* container is the bottleneck, you can't just scale that one. In that case you could decouple the containers and run three different Pods so that only the Pod that runs the *web-interface* container is duplicated.

4.17 Resources management

As we saw in the introduction, Pods and Nodes are abstractions that allow for an abstraction of memory and CPU resources. Nodes offer memory and CPU while Pods consume memory and CPU.

Kubernetes needs to ensure that Pods are effectively consuming the memory and CPU resources, and this means:

- scheduling Pods on Nodes that have enough resources to run them;
- terminating buggy Pods that consume too much memory and CPU.

Kubernetes does so thanks to the concepts of *requests* and *limits*. They are optional, but it's good practice to use them since they allow Kubernetes to correctly manage your Pods under pressure.

Requests

Requests allow your Controllers to state how much memory and CPU they need for a Pod to run. They specify a minimum that should be available on the Node where the Pod will be scheduled. When the Kubernetes scheduler needs to create a Pod, it selects a Node that has at least the memory and CPU resources stated in the *requests* section of the Controller definition.

Here is a sample definition of a Deployment:

```
apiVersion: apps/v1beta1
kind: Deployment
spec:
  template:
    spec:
      containers:
      - name: front
        image: learnbook/k8s-front:0.4
        resources:
          requests:
            cpu: "100m"
            memory: "10Mi"
```

When the Kubernetes scheduler needs to create a Pod for that Deployment, it selects a Node that has at least 10M of memory and 100 millicpus still available.

It means that if you provide values that are too high, Kubernetes may not be able to schedule your Pods, so choose wisely.

How do you decide which values to use, then? A rule of thumb is to actually run your Pods and see how much they consume under run conditions, then assign a value that is slightly higher.

Note that values are provided per container. Which means that you would provide several values to a Pod that runs several containers.

Limits

When the executable running inside a container goes
wrong, it may end up eating too much CPU and memory
resources. Limits allow you to have Kubernetes handle
that case.

When you set a limit, Kubernetes monitors resources
used by the corresponding Pods and terminates them
when used resources are actually higher than the limits
you set.

In short, limits are basically the maximum amount of CPU
and memory that you allow a Pod to use.

Here is a sample Deployment definition using limits:

```
apiVersion: apps/v1beta1
kind: Deployment
spec:
  template:
    spec:
      containers:
      - name: front
        image: learnbook/k8s-front:0.4
        resources:
          limits:
            cpu: "200m"
            memory: "50Mi"
```

Actually, the Kubernetes scheduler overcommits resources:
it doesn't immediately terminates Pods that go beyond

their assigned limits, but rather does so when the total Node resources are scarce. When this happens, the Kubernetes scheduler terminates first the Pods that most exceed their limits.

5. Exposing services

5.1 The need for services

Now that you can run Pods, you probably want them to communicate. This brings several questions that will be answered by the *Service* object.

Listen to connections from outside the cluster

When you host a server, for instance a web server, you want inbound connections from clients to reach your Pods:

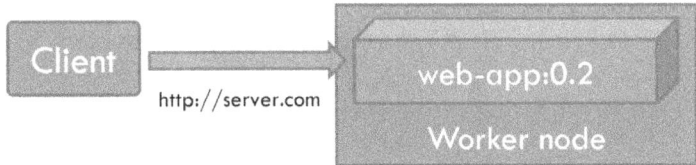

You can do so with the following command that listens to connections from outside the cluster on port 8085 and routes them to the Pods deployed by the Deployment named *name* on its 8080 port:

```
kubectl port-forward deployment/name 8085:8080
```

However, this is an imperative command and you know by now that imperative commands are not what you want for medium-term maintenance.

How can we describe the fact that the cluster should listen for connections using declarative commands? Services answer that question.

Communicate across Nodes

Since the aim of a Kubernetes cluster is to harness the power of having different Nodes running your containers, your Pods will be spread across Nodes.

A routine task (especially on microservices architectures) will be to communicate across Nodes as shown in that simplified example:

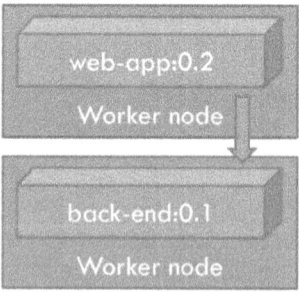

How do we communicate across Nodes? Should we keep a list of running Pods and address them? Services answer that question too.

Load-balance to multiple Pods

In order to provide high availability of your applications, it is good practice to have the same Pod duplicated across worker Nodes. We saw earlier how Deployments easily allow us to do so. But how can we ensure that inbound connections from clients will be directed to all of the Pods, as shown in the example below?

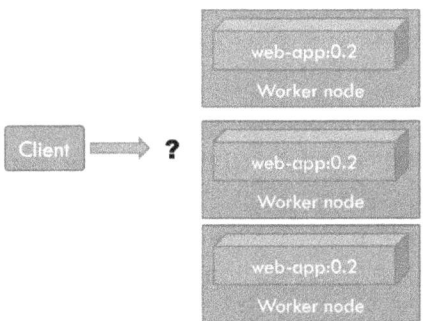

Once again, the answer is to use Services.

5.2 Services

Services are Kubernetes objects that provide answers to the three questions we just raised.

A Service object listens for incoming connections and routes them to Pods that are selected using labels, as shown below:

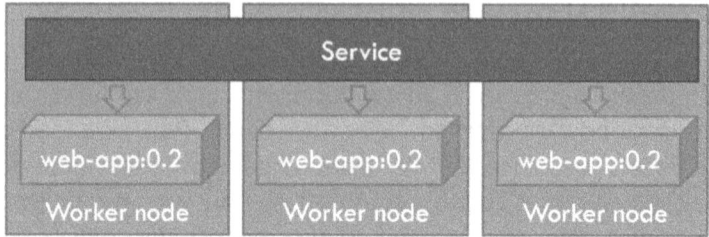

The two widely used Service types are the *LoadBalancer* and *ClusterIP* ones. The difference is whether they allow for connections from outside the cluster. Let's detail each of them.

Connections from outside the cluster

Use the *LoadBalancer* type when you create a Service, and it will route requests coming from outside the cluster to Pods that match a given selector.

Here is an example definition of a *LoadBalancer* service:

```
apiVersion: v1
kind: Service
metadata:
  name: mon-front-service
spec:
  type: LoadBalancer
  ports:
  - port: 8081
    targetPort: 80
  selector:
    app: web-app
```

When you *kubectl apply* that definition, the cluster assigns a public IP to your service. Requests made to that IP are routed to the matching Pods, as shown in the following schema:

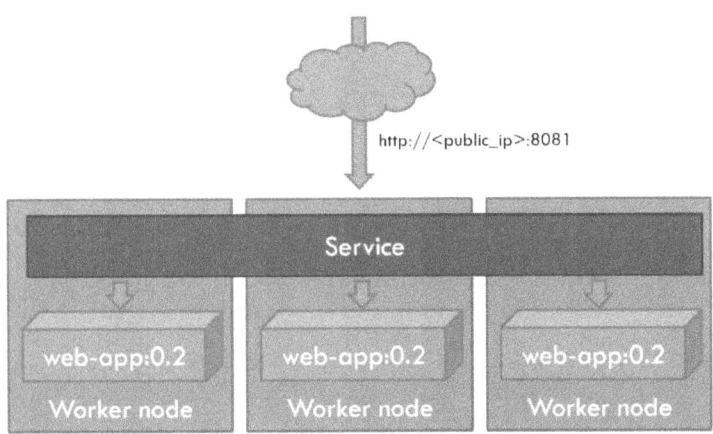

How the IP is assigned depends on the Kubernetes provider you chose when cloud-hosting your cluster, or the extensions you add to your self-managed cluster.

Let's deploy a public-facing web application as an example. Adminer is database management interface written in PHP and available as a docker image named *adminer*. In order to deploy it, I use the following two definitions:

adminer-deployment.yaml

```
apiVersion: apps/v1
kind: Deployment
metadata:
  name: adminer
spec:
  selector:
    matchLabels:
      app: adminer
  template:
    metadata:
      labels:
        app: adminer
    spec:
      containers:
      - name: adminer
        image: adminer:latest
        ports:
        - containerPort: 8080
```

adminer-service.yaml

```
apiVersion: v1
kind: Service
metadata:
  name: adminer
spec:
  type: LoadBalancer
  selector:
    app: adminer
  ports:
```

```
- port: 80
  targetPort: 8080
```

Those two definitions are applied using the following command, as you know by now:

```
kubectl apply -f .
```

The first definition actually deploys a container that runs the *adminer* application. The second definition creates a Service that exposes this application to the outside world. The following schema shows the elements we just created:

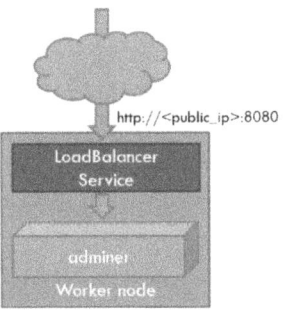

The URL used to access the service depends on the type of Kubernetes cluster that you are running:

- When running on Docker Desktop, the service is immediately available on the *localhost* address, so you can point your browser to the http://localhost URL and access the *adminer* application.

- When running on Minikube, you need to run the following command that returns the URL on which your service can be accessed:

```
minikube service mon-front-service --url
```

- When running on a PaaS cluster in the cloud, you can get the service address by running the *kubectl get services* command as shown below:

```
> kubectl get services

NAME        TYPE            CLUSTER-IP      EXTERNAL-IP
adminer     LoadBalancer    10.0.13.249     52.x.x.190
```

See the *EXTERNAL-IP* column? It gives the IP address on which the Service (and thus the *adminer* Pod) is accessible.

5.3 Exercise - Expose a web application to the internet

 Objective: deploy a web application and make it accessible from the internet.

The *learnbook/k8s-front:0.5* image is a web application that listens on its port 80. Deploy that image a Pod named *front* that has the *app=front* label. Expose that Pod using a *LoadBalancer* Service that listens on port 8080.

Open a browser and point it to http://localhost:8080 (or the public URL you obtain if running in a PaaS cluster). Make sure you can access the web application.

Once done, delete all resources created during that exercise.

5.4 Exercise solution

- Create a file named *front-deployment.yaml* with the following contents:

```
apiVersion: apps/v1beta1
kind: Deployment
metadata:
  name: front
spec:
  template:
    metadata:
      labels:
        app: front
    spec:
      containers:
      - name: front
        image: learnbook/k8s-front:0.5
```

- Create a file named *front-service.yaml* with the following contents:

```
apiVersion: v1
kind: Service
metadata:
  name: front
spec:
  type: LoadBalancer
  ports:
  - port: 8080
    targetPort: 80
  selector:
    app: front
```

- Open a command-line in the folder where you created the above files.
- Run the following commands:

```
kubectl apply -f front-deployment.yaml
kubectl apply -f front-service.yaml
kubectl get deployment
kubectl get service
```

You should get an output similar to the following one:

```
> kubectl apply -f front-deployment.yaml
deployment.apps/front created

> kubectl apply -f front-service.yaml
service/front created

> kubectl get deployment
NAME    READY   UP-TO-DATE    AVAILABLE    AGE
front   1/1     1             1            9s

> kubectl get service
NAME    TYPE           CLUSTER-IP      EXTERNAL-IP   PORT(S)
front   LoadBalancer   10.103.108.49   localhost     8080:3\
0164/TCP
```

Point your browser to the *EXTERNAL-IP* returned, in that case http://localhost:8080

Your browser should display the following page:

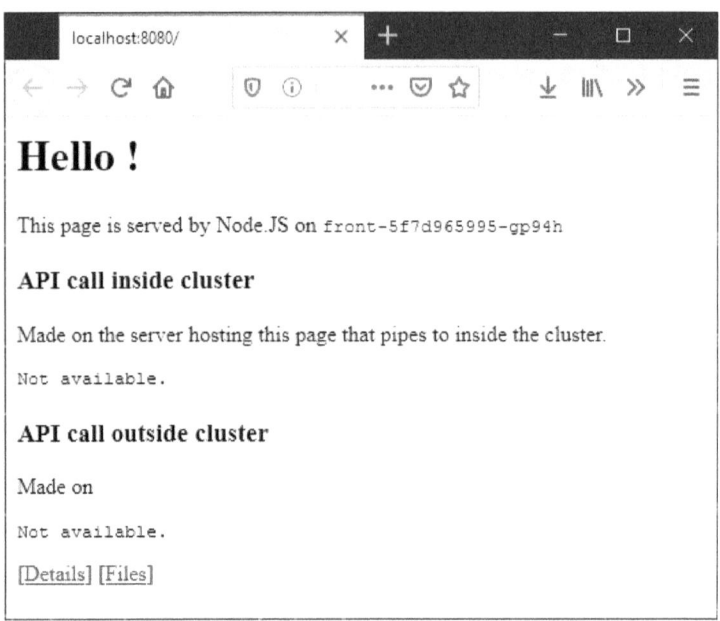

- Run the following command:

```
kubectl delete -f .
```

Connections from inside the cluster

The *ClusterIP* Service type makes Pods available to other Pods inside the cluster. Just like the *LoadBalancer* type we saw earlier, but only for services that should be available from inside the cluster.

Suppose we want to create the following application, where some *auditer* Pods need to make HTTP requests to *web-app* Pods:

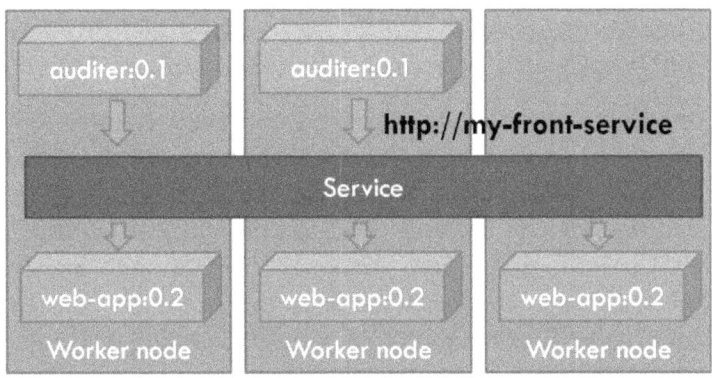

Note that such an architecture is representative of a microservices architecture where services call other services inside a cluster. It can easily be achieved using the following definition of a *ClusterIP* service:

```
apiVersion: v1
kind: Service
metadata:
  name: my-front-service
spec:
  type: ClusterIP
  ports:
  - port: 80
  selector:
    app: web-app
```

The *my-front-service* name we assign to the Service is important: a name resolution server inside the Kubernetes cluster ensures that it resolves to the actual Pods that match the *selector* defined as part of that Service. In other words, when an *auditer* Pod queries the *http://my-front-service* URL, it actually queries a *web-app* Pod.

Remember the *adminer* service I deployed in order to illustrate a LoadBalancer Service? It can query a database, so I'd like to deploy a MySQL database as another Pod. In order for the *adminer* Pod to communicate with the MySQL Pod, I can use a Service. Since that Service doesn't need to be accessed from outside the cluster, the *ClusterIP* service type is a perfect match. Here is a schema of what I want to achieve:

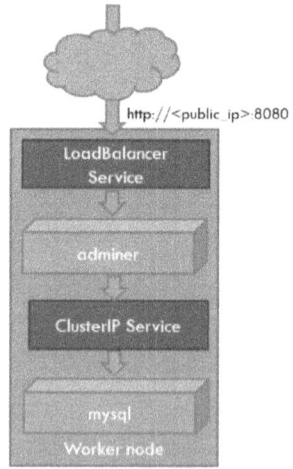

Let's deploy the components shown in the schema. For the *adminer* part, I can reuse the exact same two definitions used above:

adminer-deployment.yaml

```
apiVersion: apps/v1
kind: Deployment
metadata:
  name: adminer
spec:
  selector:
    matchLabels:
      app: adminer
  template:
    metadata:
      labels:
        app: adminer
    spec:
      containers:
      - name: adminer
        image: adminer:latest
        ports:
        - containerPort: 8080
```

adminer-service.yaml

```
apiVersion: v1
kind: Service
metadata:
  name: adminer
spec:
  type: LoadBalancer
  selector:
    app: adminer
  ports:
  - port: 80
    targetPort: 8080
```

Now, let's add two definitions for the MySQL Pod and the Service that make it available from inside the cluster:

mysql-deployment.yaml

```
apiVersion: apps/v1
kind: Deployment
metadata:
  name: mysql
spec:
  selector:
    matchLabels:
      app: mysql
  template:
    metadata:
      labels:
        app: mysql
    spec:
```

```
containers:
- name: mysql
  image: mysql:5.7
  ports:
  - containerPort: 3306
  env:
    - name: MYSQL_ROOT_PASSWORD
      value: "root"
```

Yes, that's a very insecure password. This is a demo.
Don't do this at home.

mysql-service.yaml

```
apiVersion: v1
kind: Service
metadata:
  name: mysql
spec:
  type: ClusterIP
  selector:
    app: mysql
  ports:
  - port: 3306
    targetPort: 3306
```

Those four definitions are applied to the cluster using the
kubectl apply command:

```
kubectl apply -f .
```

The *adminer* Pod can be accessed using a browser thanks to the public *LoadBalancer* Service, so I can point my browser to *http://localhost* (or *http://<public-ip>*) and get the login screen. Since the *mysql* Service exposes the MySQL Pod, it can be reached from the *adminer* Pod using the Service name: *mysql*. Which means I can use *mysql* as the address of the MySQL Server:

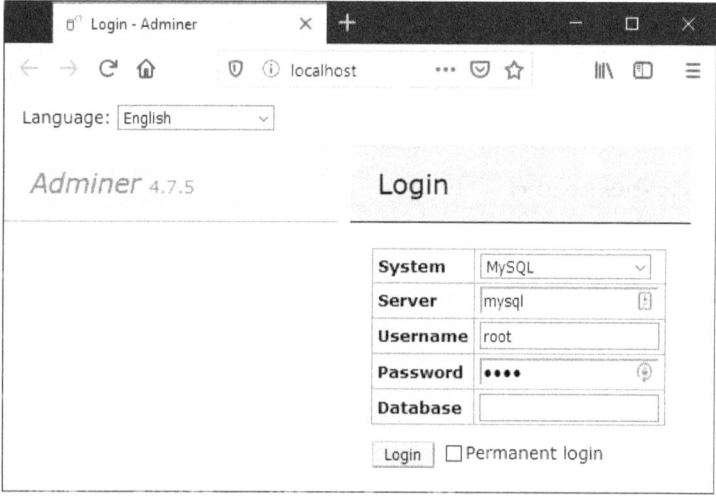

As expected, I can now access the MySQL database hosted by the *mysql* Pod:

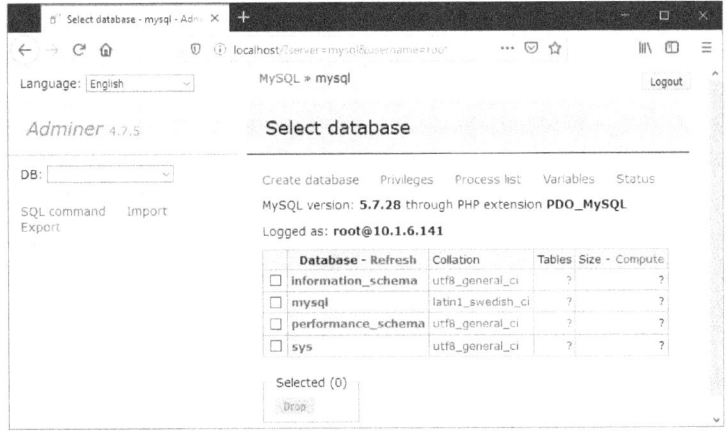

5.5 Exercise - Expose an API inside the cluster

Objective: deploy an API and make it accessible from the internet, then make it accessible to Pods that run inside the cluster.

You first need to deploy an API and make sure it is accessible from outside the cluster, in order to easily check that it is correctly deployed. We want the following application architecture at first:

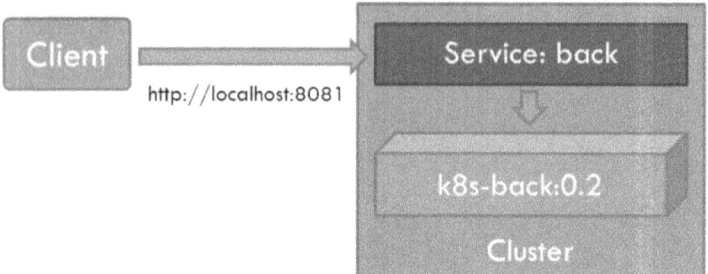

The *learnbook/k8s-back:0.2* image is an API that listens on port 80. Deploy the *learnbook/k8s-back:0.2* image as a Pod named *back* that has the *app=back* label. Expose that Pod using a *LoadBalancer* Service that listens on port 8081.

Open a browser and point it to http://localhost:8081/v1/currenttime (or the public URL you obtain if running in a PaaS cluster). Make sure you can access the API.

You now need to deploy the *front* web application and make it consume the API using its external address. The expected target application architecture will be the following:

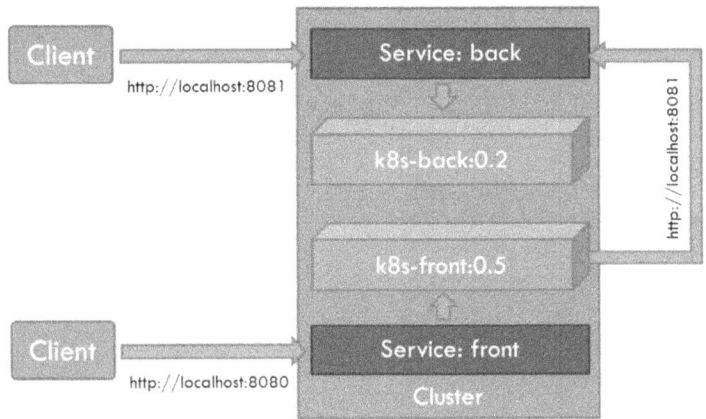

Deploy the *learnbook/k8s-front:0.5* image as a Pod named *front* that has the *app=front* label and the following environment variables:

- API_EXTERNAL_URL : http://localhost:8081
- API_CLUSTER_URL : http://back-inside

Note that the *API_EXTERNAL_URL* variable enables the front Pod to know which URL it should use to call the API. For now, the *API_CLUSTER_URL* variable does not match any endpoint; it will be used later in the exercise.

Expose the *front* Pod using a *LoadBalancer* Service that listens on port 8080.

Open a browser and point it to http://localhost:8080 (or the public URL you obtain if running in a PaaS cluster). Make sure you can access the web application. As of now, the application main page should display values in its

"API call outside cluster" zone but not in its "API call inside cluster" zone:

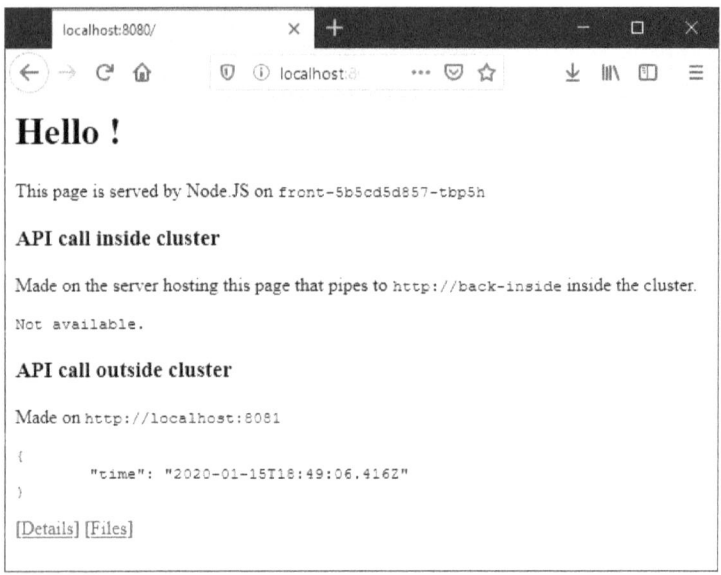

As a last step, we want the front application to call the API using an internal cluster address, not the public address. That's why we provided an internal address using the *API_CLUSTER_URL* variable. In a real world application, we would probably not call the same API from an external and internal address, but the external one was easier and that's why we began that exercise using it.

We now want to obtain the following application architecture:

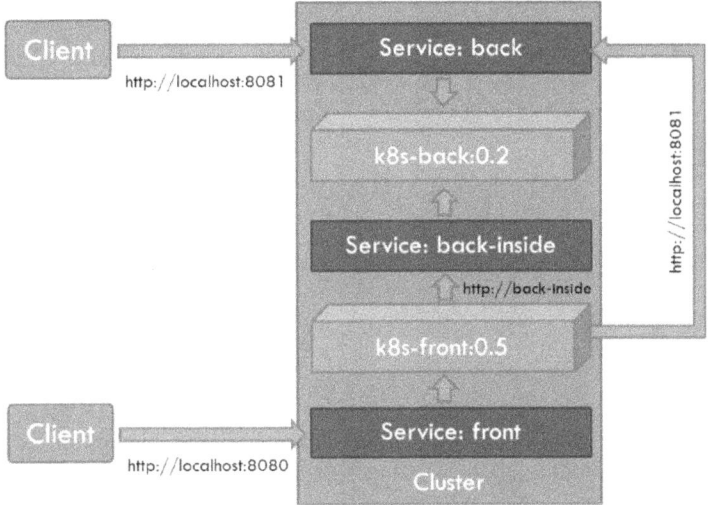

Expose the *back* Pod using a *ClusterIP* Service named *back-inside* that listens on port 80.

Open a browser and point it to http://localhost:8080 (or the public URL you obtain if running in a PaaS cluster). Make that the web application main page now displays values in both its "API call outside cluster" and "API call inside cluster" zones.

Once done, delete all resources created during that exercise.

5.6 Exercise solution

- Create a file named *back-deployment.yaml* with the following contents:

```
apiVersion: apps/v1beta1
kind: Deployment
metadata:
  name: back
spec:
  template:
    metadata:
      labels:
        app: back
    spec:
      containers:
      - name: back
        image: learnbook/k8s-back:0.2
```

- Create a file named *back-service-outside.yaml* with the following contents:

```
apiVersion: v1
kind: Service
metadata:
  name: back-outside
spec:
  type: LoadBalancer
  ports:
  - port: 8081
    targetPort: 80
  selector:
    app: back
```

- Open a command-line in the folder where you created the above files.
- Run the following commands:

```
kubectl apply -f back-deployment.yaml
kubectl apply -f back-service-outside.yaml
kubectl get deployment
kubectl get service
```

You should get an output similar to the following one:

```
> kubectl apply -f back-deployment.yaml
deployment.apps/back created

> kubectl apply -f back-service-outside.yaml
service/back-outside created

> kubectl get deployment
NAME    READY   UP-TO-DATE   AVAILABLE   AGE
back    1/1     1            1           55s

> kubectl get service
NAME           TYPE           EXTERNAL-IP   PORT(S)
back-outside   LoadBalancer   localhost     8081:31388/TCP
```

Point your browser to the *EXTERNAL-IP* returned plus
/v1/currenttime, in that case http://localhost:8081/v1/currenttime

Your browser should display the resulting JSON:

- Create a file named *front-deployment.yaml* with the following contents:

```
apiVersion: apps/v1beta1
kind: Deployment
metadata:
  name: front
spec:
  template:
    metadata:
      labels:
        app: front
    spec:
      containers:
      - name: front
        image: learnbook/k8s-front:0.5
        env:
        - name: API_EXTERNAL_URL
          value: "http://localhost:8081"
        - name: API_CLUSTER_URL
          value: "http://back-inside"
```

- Create a file named *front-service.yaml* with the following contents (that one is the same as in the previous exercise):

```
apiVersion: v1
kind: Service
metadata:
  name: front
spec:
  type: LoadBalancer
  ports:
  - port: 8080
    targetPort: 80
  selector:
    app: front
```

- Open a command-line in the folder where you created the above files.
- Run the following commands:

```
kubectl apply -f front-deployment.yaml
kubectl apply -f front-service.yaml
kubectl get deployment
kubectl get service
```

You should get an output similar to the following one:

```
> kubectl apply -f front-deployment.yaml
deployment.apps/front created
```

```
> kubectl apply -f front-service.yaml
service/front created
```

```
> kubectl get deployment
NAME     READY   UP-TO-DATE   AVAILABLE   AGE
back     1/1     1            1           23m
front    1/1     1            1           50s
```

```
> kubectl get service
NAME            TYPE           EXTERNAL-IP   PORT(S)
back-outside    LoadBalancer   localhost     8081:31388/TCP
front           LoadBalancer   localhost     8080:31594/TCP
```

Point your browser to the *EXTERNAL-IP* returned, in that case http://localhost:8080

Your browser should display the following page:

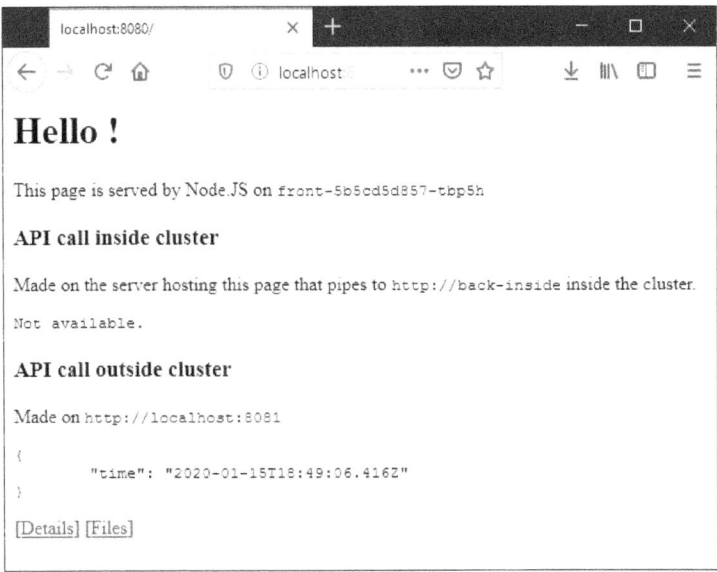

- Create a file named *back-service-inside.yaml* with the following contents (that one is the same as in the previous exercise):

```
apiVersion: v1
kind: Service
metadata:
  name: back-inside
spec:
  type: ClusterIP
  ports:
    - port: 80
  selector:
    app: back
```

- Open a command-line in the folder where you created the above file.
- Run the following commands:

```
kubectl apply -f back-service-inside.yaml
kubectl get services
```

You should get an output similar to the following one:

```
> kubectl apply -f back-service-inside.yaml
service/back-inside created

> kubectl get service
NAME          TYPE          EXTERNAL-IP  PORT(S)
back-inside   ClusterIP     <none>       80/TCP
back-outside  LoadBalancer  localhost    8081:31388/TCP
front         LoadBalancer  localhost    8080:31594/TCP
```

In your browser, look again at the page that displays http://localhost:8080

Your browser should have the following display (note that the "API call inside cluster" zone is now populated):

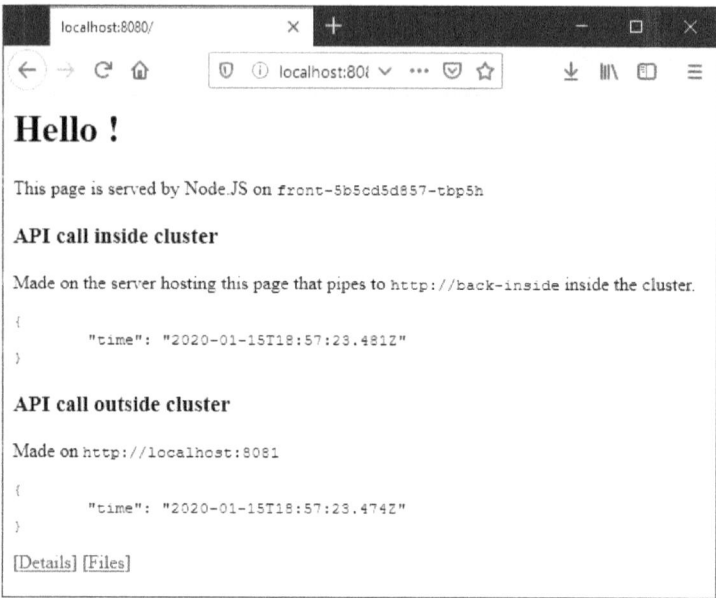

- Run the following command:

```
kubectl delete -f .
```

5.7 Ingress

An Ingress is a Kubernetes object used to add extra power to Services. Ingresses add an extra layer between inbound connections and Services. They are an abstraction for reverse proxies.

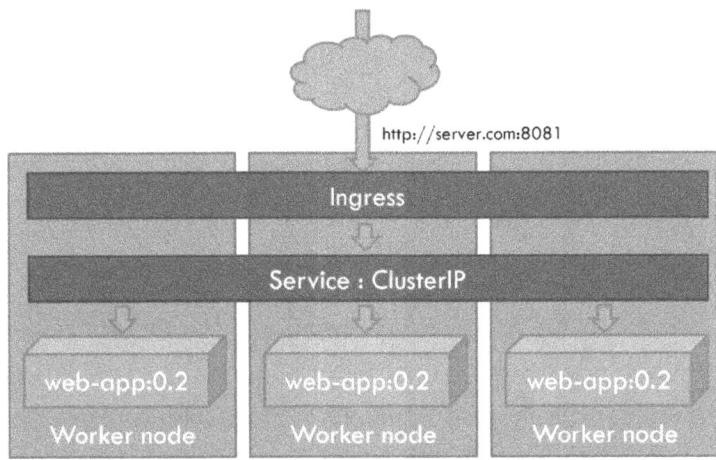

Some of the benefits of using Ingresses are:

- Route incoming requests to different Services according to the incoming URL. For instance, you could use similar URLs to route users to different versions of an application:
  - http://front/store could route to a *store:1.0* application;
  - http://front/old/store could route to a *store:0.8* application.
- Add TLS between incoming requests and your Services in order to secure connections to your cluster (in short, https:// addresses instead of http:// ones), managing certificates and encryption in a common Ingress Controller.
- Manage your own load balancing service.

Ingress objects are declared in your Kubernetes cluster, but the actual functionality is provided by an Ingress Controller. You can deploy and manage your Ingress Controller of choice, for instance:

- nginx-ingress
- contour
- traefik
- PaaS controllers when running in the Cloud.

Note that the ingress controllers are based on reverse-proxy software. This is totally normal since Ingress objects are abstractions for reverse proxies.

Once an Ingress Controller is deployed to your Kubernetes cluster, you can add as many Ingress objects as you wish. The Ingress Controller will scan the Ingress objects in order to know which services it should provide.

This is how you declare a simple Ingress object:

```
apiVersion: extensions/v1beta1
kind: Ingress
metadata:
  name: frontandback-ingress
spec:
  rules:
    - host: server.com
      http:
        paths:
          - path: /app
```

```
backend:
  serviceName: web-app
  servicePort: 80
```

Thanks to the above Ingress object, the Ingress Controller will know that an incoming http://server.com/app request should be routed to the Service named *web-app*. That service can be a *ClusterIP* type service.

6. Volumes

6.1 The need for volumes

Changes made to the file system inside a container are ephemeral. Once the container stops, they are lost unless you take some steps to make them persist elsewhere. Containers are more easily managed when they are stateless, but you will need to persist data at some point.

Persistence needs depend on your applications. Persisted data may be shared across containers in the same Pod, or shared across several containers from different Pods on a Worker Node, or even shared among containers that run on different Worker Nodes.

You could try and persist data on the file system of the Worker Nodes, but from a Kubernetes point of view Nodes are interchangeable and a Pod may be restarted on another Worker Node for many reasons. Also, how would you manage sharing data to other Pods running on different Nodes?

Kubernetes provides an abstraction model for persistent storage, in the same way that it provides an abstraction model for memory and CPU resources. You know by now that Pods make memory and CPU requests while Nodes

127

offer memory and CPU. The same goes with persistent storage: Pods make requests for Volumes, and volume providers offer persistent storage.

A Pod may make any of two request types:

- Volume: its duration is limited to that of the Pod that declares it.
- PersistentVolumeClaim: an object that lives inde-pendently from Pods, so it can live longer than Pods.

Let's see both in more details.

6.2 Short-lived storage with Volumes

A Volume is declared by a Pod. All of the containers running inside a Pod can see the Volume. The Volume lives only as long as the declaring Pod.

It may look like Volumes are short-lived, but that is only partly true. The Volume object is short lived just like its declaring Pod, but it can rely on storage that persists for much longer. For instance, if a Volume uses an external storage type like an *Azure Disk*, its data is persisted and may be read later by another Pod that attaches its Volume to the same storage. Actually, most storage types that can be used by Volumes are persistent.

Anyway, a short-lived storage that is scoped to a Pod may also be useful if you want to exchange data between containers running inside the same Pod, as illustrated by this chapter's exercise.

Here is a Volume declaration for a Pod:

```
apiVersion: apps/v1beta1
kind: Deployment
spec:
  template:
    spec:
      volumes:
        - name: persistent-data
          emptyDir: {}
      containers:
        - name: front
          image: my-image:1.0
          volumeMounts:
            - mountPath: /external
              name: persistent-data
```

As you can see, the Volume is declared within a Pod and mounted on the Pod's containers. The *front* container sees the Volume as its */external* folder.

In the above example, the Volume type is *emptyDir*. It's a short-lived, non-reliable storage that can be read from and written to, and may be stored in memory or onto the Worker Node's disk.

The following Volume types are available as of writing (full list here[1]):

---
[1] https://kubernetes.io/docs/concepts/storage/volumes/#types-of-volumes

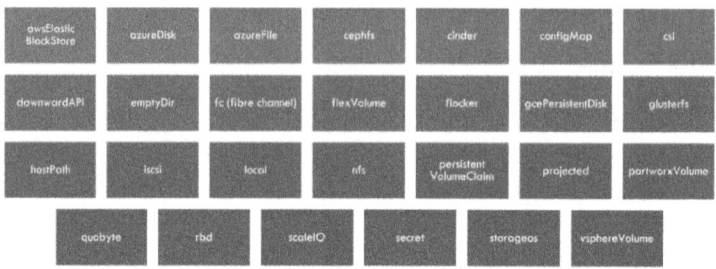

You can see that there are traditional types like *nfs* and *hostPath* that enable writing to well-known disk systems, but also distributed persistent storage tailored for clusters like *glusterfs* and *flocker*. There are also the *configMap* and *secret* types that refer to Kubernetes objects we will see in the Configuration chapter; those enable you to see configuration data as files from your containers.

Some Volume types need extra information when declared. For instance, the *azureDisk* type needs you to specify the URI of the disks it actually refers to:

```
apiVersion: apps/v1beta1
kind: Deployment
spec:
  template:
    spec:
      volumes:
        - name: persistent-data
          azureDisk:
            diskName: test.vhd
            diskURI: https://...oft.net/vhds/test.vhd
      containers:
```

```
- name: front
  image: my-image:1.0
  volumeMounts:
    - mountPath: /external
      name: persistent-data
```

6.3 Exercise - Create and use a Volume

 Objective: create and use an *emptyDir* type Volume in order to share files between containers that run in the same Pod.

The *learnbook/k8s-creator:0.2* image creates files with a random name in its directory named */shared*. The *learnbook/k8s-front:0.5* image lists files that are located in its own directory named */shared*.

You should run those two images as two containers inside the same Pod, and create a Volume of type *emptyDir* inside the Pod. Make sure that both containers use the same Volume, so that files written by one container are consumed by the other.

You should aim for the following target architecture:

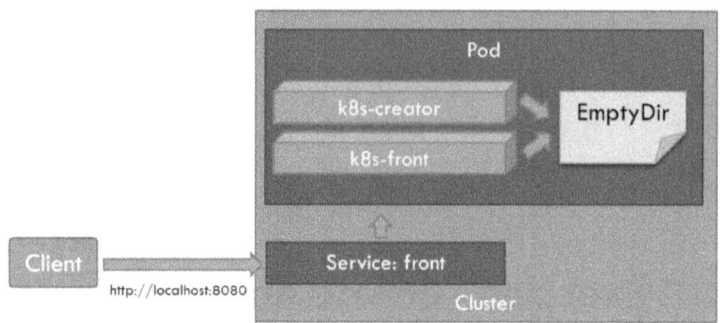

Create a Deployment that hosts the *learnbook/k8s-creator:0.2* and *learnbook/k8s-front:0.5* images in the same Pod. Expose the *front* application from the Pod using a *LoadBalancer* Service that listens on port 8080.

Open a browser and point it to http://localhost:8080/files (or the public URL you obtain if running in a PaaS cluster). There is no file in the folder. Explain why.

Add an *emptyDir* type Volume in the Pod, and make sure it is exposed to the *front* and *creator* containers.

Open a browser and point it to http://localhost:8080/files. Files should be displayed as you refresh the page.

Delete all resources created during that exercise.

Recreate the same Pod using the same containers, same Volume and same Service.

Open a browser and point it to http://localhost:8080/files. There are no files anymore. Explain why.

6.4 Exercise solution

- Create a file named *front-deployment.yaml1* with the following contents:

```
apiVersion: apps/v1beta1
kind: Deployment
metadata:
  name: front
spec:
  template:
    metadata:
      labels:
        app: front
    spec:
      containers:
      - name: front
        image: learnbook/k8s-front:0.3
      - name: creator
        image: learnbook/k8s-creator:0.2
```

- Create a file named *front-service.yaml* with the following contents:

```
apiVersion: v1
kind: Service
metadata:
  name: front
spec:
  type: LoadBalancer
  ports:
  - port: 8080
    targetPort: 80
  selector:
    app: front
```

- Open a command-line in the folder where you created the above files.
- Run the following commands:

```
kubectl apply -f front-deployment1.yaml
kubectl apply -f front-service.yaml
kubectl get service
```

You should get an output similar to the following one:

```
> kubectl apply -f front-deployment1.yaml

deployment.apps/front created

> kubectl apply -f front-service.yaml

service/front created

> kubectl get deployment

NAME    READY   UP-TO-DATE   AVAILABLE   AGE
front   1/1     1            1           97s

> kubectl get service

NAME    TYPE           CLUSTER-IP     EXTERNAL-IP   PORT(S)
front   LoadBalancer   10.102.58.78   localhost     8080:30\
221/TCP
```

Point your browser to the *EXTERNAL-IP* returned, in that case http://localhost:8080/files. You should get a page similar to the following one:

The displayed page doesn't list any file. This is due to the fact that the *creator* container creates files in a */shared* directory which is local to the *creator* container itself. The */shared* directory of the *front* container that we see listed is another directory, local to the *front* container.

- Create a file named *front-deployment.yaml2* with the following contents:

```
apiVersion: apps/v1beta1
kind: Deployment
metadata:
  name: front
spec:
  template:
    metadata:
      labels:
        app: front
    spec:
      volumes:
```

```
     - name: shared
       emptyDir: {}
   containers:
   - name: front
     image: learnbook/k8s-front:0.3
     volumeMounts:
       - mountPath: /shared
         name: shared
   - name: creator
     image: learnbook/k8s-creator:0.2
     volumeMounts:
       - mountPath: /shared
         name: shared
```

- Open a command-line in the folder where you created the above files.
- Run the following command:

```
kubectl apply -f front-deployment2.yaml
```

You should get an output similar to the following one:

```
> kubectl apply -f front-deployment2.yaml

deployment.apps/front configured
```

Refresh the http://localhost:8080/files page in your browser.
Your browser should display a page similar to that one:

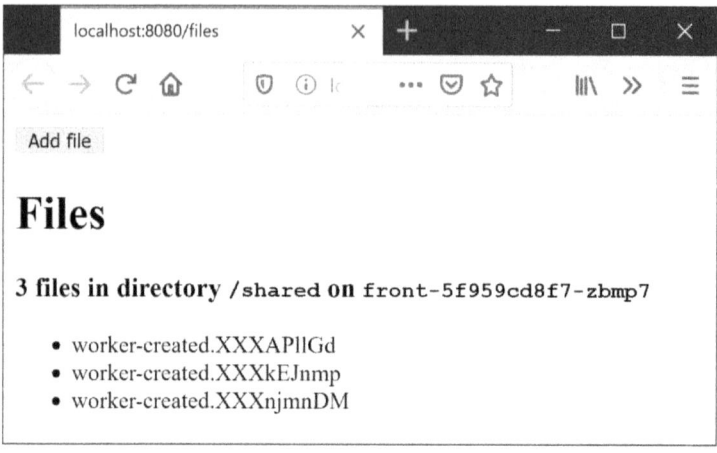

- Run the following commands:

```
kubectl delete -f .
kubectl apply -f front-deployment2.yaml
kubectl apply -f front-service.yaml
```

You should get an output similar to the following one:

```
> kubectl delete -f .

deployment.apps "front" deleted
service "front" deleted

> kubectl apply -f front-deployment2.yaml

deployment.apps/front created

> kubectl apply -f front-service.yaml

service/front created
```

Refresh the http://localhost:8080/files page in your browser. Your browser should display a page without any files (or with few files if you waited long enough before refreshing the page). This is due to the fact that the *emptyDir* Volume holding the previously created files was attached to the Pod, but you deleted and recreated the Pod.

- Run the following command:

```
kubectl delete -f .
```

6.5 Persistent storage with PersistentVolumeClaims

Consuming persistent storage

In order to handle persistent storage that you can share between Pods and across Worker Nodes, Kubernetes provides the *PersistentVolumeClaim* object.

A PersistentVolumeClaim object exists in your cluster independently from any Pod, and points to an actual storage endpoint which is the *PersistentVolume*:

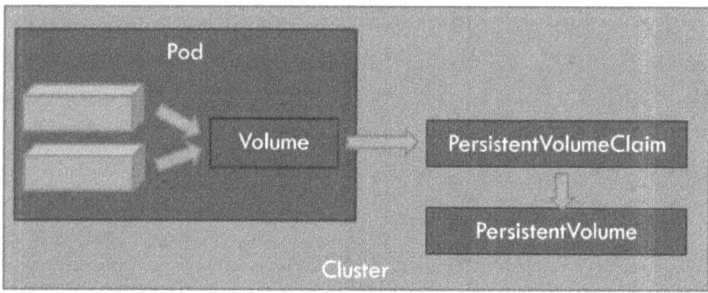

PersistentVolumes are provisioned by those administering the Kubernetes cluster, either "manually" or using dynamically assigned PersistentVolumes (see Providing persistent storage).

The PersistentVolumes mechanics isn't complex just for the sake of complexity: those objects provide you with an abstraction layer that completely decouples the storage needs (consumed by the Devs) from the actual storage providers (provisioned by the Ops). In fact, a PersistentVolumeClaim consumes part of a PersistentVolume just like a Pod consumes part of a Node.

For Devs, consuming a piece of a PersistentVolume is a two-step process: first you create a PersistentVolumeClaim, next you hook that PersistentVolumeClaim to your Pod just like you would mount a plain Volume. Here are the two objects:

PersistentVolumeClaim declaration

```
apiVersion: v1
kind: PersistentVolumeClaim
metadata:
  name: claiming-disk
spec:
  accessModes:
    - ReadWriteOnce
  resources:
    requests:
      storage: 1Gi
```

**Declaration of a Deployment where the Pod consumes a Persis-
tentVolumeClaim**

```
apiVersion: apps/v1beta1
kind: Deployment
spec:
  template:
    spec:
      volumes:
        - name: persistent-data
          persistentVolumeClaim:
            claimName: claiming-disk
      containers:
        - name: front
          image: my-image:1.0
          volumeMounts:
            - mountPath: /external
              name: persistent-data
```

Providing persistent storage

There are two ways a PersistentVolumeClaim actually
gets persistent storage, and it is up to the Ops to decide
for a strategy.

The first one is for the cluster's administrator to create
PersistentVolumes, which will be consumed by the Per-
sistentVolumeClaims.

The second one is to specify a StorageClass on the PersistentVolumeClaim, which allows for dynamic creation
of Volumes.

At the time of writing, the following storage classes are available:

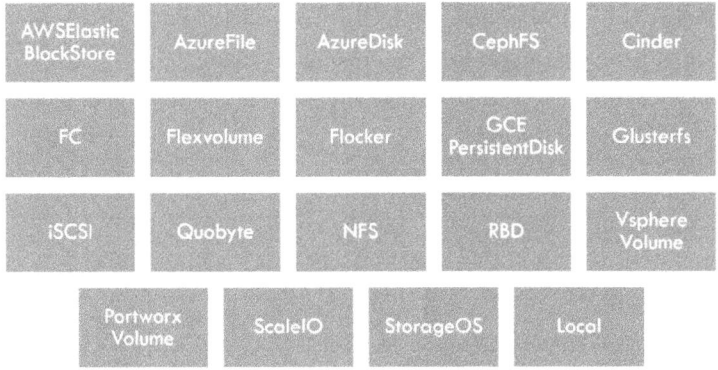

6.6 Exercise - Create and use a PersistentVolume

Objective: use a PersistentVolume to persist files even when a Pod dies.

Use the Deployment from the previous exercise but replace the *emptyDir* with a reference to a PersistentVolumeClaim that you create.

Open a browser and point it to http://localhost:8080/files (or the public URL you obtain if running in a PaaS cluster). Files should be displayed as you refresh the page.

Delete the Deployment and Service. Refresh the browser: the page is unavailable.

Recreate the Deployment and Service.

Refresh the browser. The previous files should still be displayed as you refresh the page. They weren't lost as the Pod was deleted.

Delete all resources created.

6.7 Exercise solution

- Create a file named *persistentvolumeclaim.yaml* with the following contents:

```
apiVersion: v1
kind: PersistentVolumeClaim
metadata:
  name: shared-on-disk
spec:
  accessModes:
    - ReadWriteOnce
  resources:
    requests:
      storage: 1Gi
```

- Reuse the file named *front-deployment.yaml* from the previous exercise, modifying the *volumes* section in order to get the following contents:

```
apiVersion: apps/v1beta1
kind: Deployment
metadata:
  name: front
spec:
  template:
    metadata:
      labels:
        app: front
    spec:
      volumes:
        # - name: shared
        #   emptyDir: {}
        - name: shared
          persistentVolumeClaim:
            claimName: shared-on-disk
      containers:
      - name: front
        image: learnbook/k8s-front:0.3
        volumeMounts:
          - mountPath: /shared
            name: shared
      - name: creator
        image: learnbook/k8s-creator:0.2
        volumeMounts:
          - mountPath: /shared
            name: shared
```

- Reuse the file named *front-service.yaml* from the previous exercise, with the following contents:

```
apiVersion: v1
kind: Service
metadata:
  name: front
spec:
  type: LoadBalancer
  ports:
  - port: 8080
    targetPort: 80
  selector:
    app: front
```

- Open a command-line in the folder where you created the above files.
- Run the following commands:

```
kubectl apply -f persistentvolumeclaim.yaml
kubectl apply -f front-deployment.yaml
kubectl apply -f front-service.yaml
```

You should get an output similar to the following one:

```
> kubectl apply -f persistentvolumeclaim.yaml

persistentvolumeclaim/shared-on-disk created

> kubectl apply -f front-deployment.yaml

deployment.apps/front created

> kubectl apply -f front-service.yaml

service/front created
```

Point your browser to http://localhost:8080/files. You should get a page similar to the following one:

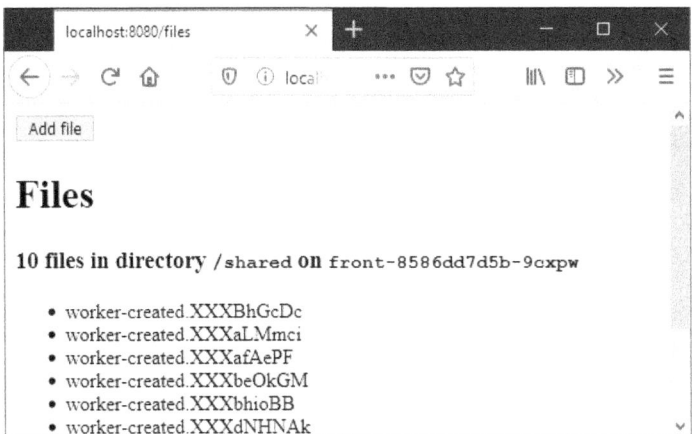

• In the command-line, run the following commands:

```
kubectl delete -f front-deployment.yaml
kubectl delete -f front-service.yaml
kubectl apply -f front-deployment.yaml
kubectl apply -f front-service.yaml
```

You should get an output similar to the following one:

```
> kubectl delete -f front-deployment.yaml

deployment.apps "front" deleted

> kubectl delete -f front-service.yaml

service "front" deleted

> kubectl apply -f front-deployment.yaml

deployment.apps/front created

> kubectl apply -f front-service.yaml

service/front created
```

Refresh the http://localhost:8080/files page in your browser. Your browser should display a page similar to that one:

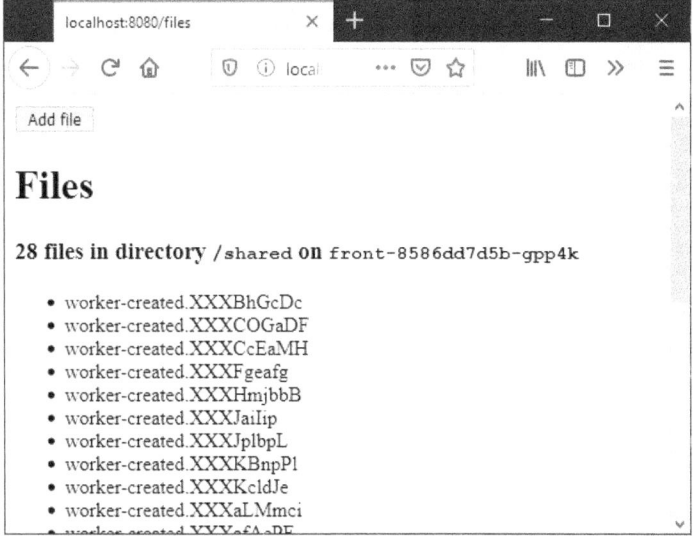

Note that the files that were visible from the previous step are still visible, in spite of the fact that the Pod was deleted and recreated.

- Run the following command:

```
kubectl delete -f .
```

I need you, super-hero!

Thank you so much for reading this book. I do hope that it helps you understand and get confident with Kubernetes.

As a reader, you are kind of a super-hero: you gain the power to package and deploy your applications seamlessly over clusters and make computers more useful.

Guess what? You have another superpower: to rate this book on the site where you purchased it. You may feel it's nothing, but it is super important for auto-edited books like this one. Please, take some minutes of your precious time to rate this book. That counts a lot for independent authors like myself!

7. Configuration

7.1 Similar but different

Whatever the programming language inside your Pods, your containers are likely to need runtime parameters dependent on their configuration. For instance, the address of a database to connect to or some credentials. The *ConfigMap* and *Secret* Kubernetes objects make such information a first-class citizen in a cluster.

As such, both objects can be managed with the common *kubectl* commands we saw for Pods, Deployments and Services. For instance you would get a list of all the ConfigMap objects using the following command:

```
kubectl get configmaps
```

Both *ConfigMap* and *Secret* are very similar, although *Secret* will be preferred over *ConfigMap* for more sensitive information. Let's see about both.

7.2 Configmap

Declaration

A ConfigMap stores key / value pairs that will be made available to any number of Pods across Nodes. Those keys and their values can be consumed by Pods as any of those options:

- environment variables defined for all entries;
- environment variables defined for some entries;
- files.

At the moment of declaring a ConfigMap, you don't need to know how it will be exposed to Pods. Here is an example definition:

```
apiVersion: v1
kind: ConfigMap
metadata:
  name: configmap-values
data:
  key1: "value1"
  key2: "value2"
```

In the definition above, there are two entries. The *key1* entry has the *value1* value, while the *key2* entry has the *value2* value.

As stated above, there are three ways to consume those keys from a Pod.

Consume as files

Remember the Volumes used for persistent storage? A *ConfigMap* object can be mounted as a Volume inside a Pod. That means that each of its keys is seen as a read-only file; the contents of each file are the values assigned to the keys.

Most programming languages can read their configuration from files, so most containers expect such configuration files. ConfigMap objects can be used for this, and this means that the configuration data can come from a single YAML file.

As an example, let's mount the ConfigMap shown earlier into a Pod:

```
apiVersion: apps/v1beta1
kind: Deployment
spec:
  template:
    spec:
      volumes:
        - name: config-volume
          configMap:
            name: configmap-values
      containers:
      - name: front
        image: learnbook/k8s-front:0.4
        volumeMounts:
          - mountPath: /config
            name: config-volume
```

This is the exact same syntax we used for Volumes, but the Volume type is *configMap*. You can see that the *front* container mounts the Volume as its */config* path; as a result, the *front* container sees the following file:

File name	File contents
/config/key1	value1
/config/key2	value2

Note that the syntax allows each container to mount the same Volume in a different path, to better suit the container's needs.

Consume as environment variables

Many containers need their parameters to be provided as environment variables. This is easily done when configuration is stored as a ConfigMap object.

Consider the following ConfigMap definition:

```
apiVersion: apps/v1beta1
kind: Deployment
spec:
  template:
    spec:
      containers:
      - name: front
        image: learnbook/k8s-front:0.4
        envFrom:
          - configMapRef:
              name: configmap-values
```

The *envFrom* entry means that all of the keys from the ConfigMap named *configmap-values* will be exposed to the container as environment variables with the same names. Considering the *configmap-values* ConfigMap we defined, the *front* container will see the following environment variables:

Variable name	Variable value
key1	value1
key2	value2

Consume as select environment variables

There are cases where you want to provide environment variables to a container, but you don't want to expose all of the entries from a ConfigMap, or you want to provide them under specific variable names. There is a more verbose syntax for doing so, where you state each key that you want to expose and the name of the environment variable to which its value will be assigned.

Consider the following definition:

```
apiVersion: apps/v1beta1
kind: Deployment
spec:
  template:
    spec:
      containers:
      - name: front
        image: learnbook/k8s-front:0.4
        env:
        - name: VAR_NAME
          valueFrom:
            configMapKeyRef:
              name: configmap-values
              key: key2
```

It creates a Pod and exposes a single ConfigMap value as a single environment variable. The *key2* entry from the ConfigMap named *configmap-values* is seen as an environment variable named *VAR_NAME*. You can repeat the *env/name* entry as much as needed to create as many environment variables as needed.

Considering the definition we just saw, the *front* container will see the following environment variable:

Variable name	Variable value
VAR_NAME	value2

7.3 Exercise - Create and use a ConfigMap

 Objective: create a ConfigMap and consume it in different ways from a Pod.

We aim for the following architecture:

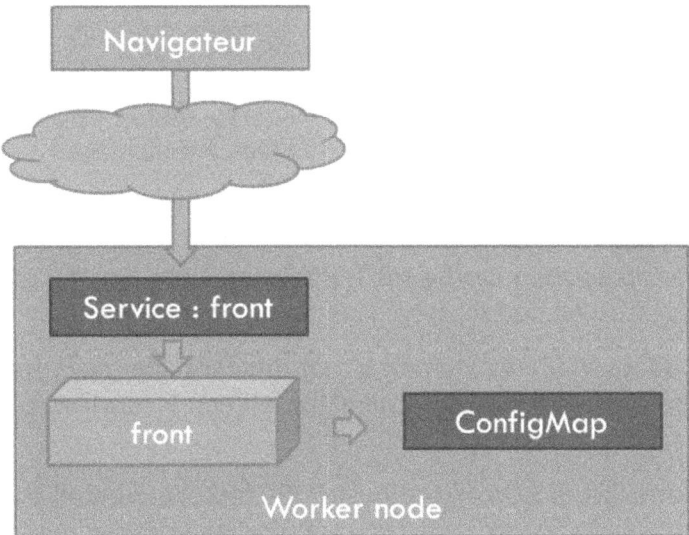

Create a ConfigMap object with the following entries:

Key	Value
message	"Hello world"
config	"Debug"
magicNumber	"42"

Create a Deployment for the *learnbook/k8s-front:0.4* image and expose it with a LoadBalancer Service.

Display the http://localhost:8080/files URL in your browser (it shows the names of all the files located in the */shared* folder of the container). No file should appear.

Update the Deployment so that the container sees the ConfigMap object as files in its */shared* directory.

Refresh the http://localhost:8080/files page in your browser. The three entries from the ConfigMap should be shown (note that only the names of the files are displayed).

Display the http://localhost:8080/details URL in your browser (it shows the names of all the environment variables seen by the the container). Note that there is no entry named *message*, *config* or *magicNumber*.

Update the Deployment so that the container sees all of the entries from the ConfigMap object as environment variables.

Refresh the http://localhost:8080/details page in your browser. The three entries from the ConfigMap should be shown.

Delete all resources created.

7.4 Exercise solution

- Create a file named *commonvalues-configmap.yaml* with the following contents:

```
apiVersion: v1
kind: ConfigMap
metadata:
  name: common-values
data:
  message: "Hello world"
  config: "Debug"
  magicNumber: "42"
```

- Create a file named *front-deployment1.yaml* with the following contents:

```
apiVersion: apps/v1beta1
kind: Deployment
metadata:
  name: front
spec:
  template:
    metadata:
      labels:
        app: front
    spec:
```

```
containers:
- name: front
  image: learnbook/k8s-front:0.4
```

- Create a file named *front-service.yaml* with the following contents:

```
apiVersion: v1
kind: Service
metadata:
  name: front
spec:
  type: LoadBalancer
  ports:
  - port: 8080
    targetPort: 80
  selector:
    app: front
```

- Open a command-line in the folder where you created the above files.
- Run the following commands:

```
kubectl apply -f commonvalues-configmap.yaml
kubectl apply -f front-deployment1.yaml
kubectl apply -f front-service.yaml
kubectl get cm
kubectl describe cm common-values
```

You should get an output similar to the following one:

```
> kubectl apply -f commonvalues-configmap.yaml

configmap/common-values created

> kubectl apply -f front-deployment1.yaml

deployment.apps/front created

> kubectl apply -f front-service.yaml

service/front created

> kubectl get cm

NAME              DATA    AGE
common-values     3       40s

> kubectl describe cm common-values

Name:           common-values
Namespace:      default
Labels:         <none>
Annotations:    ...
```

```
Data
====
config:
- - - -
Debug
magicNumber:
- - - -
42
message:
- - - -
Hello world
Events:    <none>
```

Point your browser to http://localhost:8080/files. You should get a page similar to the following one:

- Create a file named *front-deployment2.yaml* by adding some entries to the *front-deployment1.yaml*. The *front-deployment2.yaml* should have the following contents:

```
apiVersion: apps/v1beta1
kind: Deployment
metadata:
  name: front
spec:
  template:
    metadata:
      labels:
        app: front
    spec:
      volumes:
        - name: shared
          configMap:
            name: common-values
      containers:
      - name: front
        image: learnbook/k8s-front:0.4
        volumeMounts:
          - mountPath: /shared
            name: shared
```

- In the command-line, run the following command:

```
kubectl apply -f front-deployment2.yaml
```

You should get an output similar to the following one:

```
> kubectl apply -f front-deployment2.yaml

deployment.apps/front configured
```

Refresh the http://localhost:8080/files page in your browser.
Your browser should display a page similar to that one:

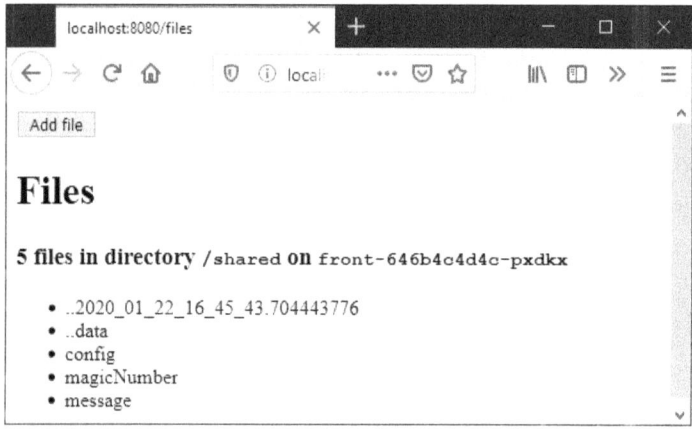

Point your browser to http://localhost:8080/details. You
should get a page similar to the following one:

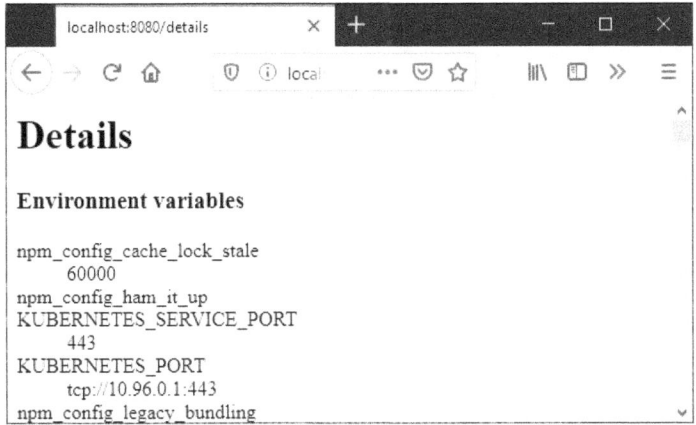

No entry named *message*, *config* or *magicNumber* is displayed on the page.

- Create a file named *front-deployment4.yaml* by adding some entries to the *front-deployment1.yaml*. The *front-deployment4.yaml* should have the following contents:

```
apiVersion: apps/v1beta1
kind: Deployment
metadata:
  name: front
spec:
  template:
    metadata:
      labels:
        app: front
    spec:
```

```
containers:
- name: front
  image: learnbook/k8s-front:0.4
  envFrom:
    - configMapRef:
        name: common-values
```

- In the command-line, run the following command:

```
kubectl apply -f front-deployment4.yaml
```

You should get an output similar to the following one:

```
> kubectl apply -f front-deployment4.yaml

deployment.apps/front configured
```

Refresh the http://localhost:8080/details page in your browser. Your browser should display a page similar to that one:

The three entries from the ConfigMap are shown when you scroll the page (the screenshot above shows the *message* variable).

- Run the following command:

```
kubectl delete -f .
```

7.5 Secret

Secrets are very similar to ConfigMap objects, and offer a few extra features geared toward storing information that needs to be secured.

Secrets add an extra level of security but they are far from very secure. You need to make sure that only the appropriate users or Pods can access them; this is done by assigning the correct roles to User and ServiceAccount objects (see RBAC). Also be aware that they don't provide for auditing or access control checks at a glance that some regulations may require your cluster to conform to. Secrets may be "good enough" security solution for simple needs, but for secure secrets management you will need more robust solutions like Azure Key Vault.

A Secret may be created using a configuration file:

```
apiVersion: v1
kind: Secret
metadata:
  name: secret-values
stringData:
  key1: "secret value1"
  key2: "secret value2"
```

 If the secret data isn't encrypted, you probably don't want it to appear in a clear text file like the one above. You are better off using the *kubectl create secret* command to create them.

Using a Secret in a Pod is exactly like using a ConfigMap:

you can consume it as environment variables or files, as shown in the following definitions.

Consuming a secret as files

```
apiVersion: apps/v1beta1
kind: Deployment
spec:
  template:
    spec:
      volumes:
        - name: config-volume
          secret:
            secretName: secret-values
      containers:
        - name: front
          image: learnbook/k8s-front:0.4
          volumeMounts:
            - mountPath: /config
              name: config-volume
```

Consuming a secret as environment variables

```
apiVersion: apps/v1beta1
kind: Deployment
spec:
  template:
    spec:
      containers:
        - name: front
          image: learnbook/k8s-front:0.4
          envFrom:
```

```
  - secretRef:
      name: secret-values
```

Consuming a secret as a named environment variable

```
apiVersion: apps/v1beta1
kind: Deployment
spec:
  template:
    spec:
      containers:
        - name: front
          image: learnbook/k8s-front:0.4
          env:
            - name: VAR_NAME
              valueFrom:
                secretKeyRef:
                  name: secret-values
                  key: key2
```

7.6 Exercise - Create and use a Secret

 Objective: create a Secret and consume it in
different ways from a Pod.

Create a Secret object with the following entries:

Key	Value
message	"Hello secret world"
config	"Hidden"
magicNumber	"0"

Create a Deployment for the *learnbook/k8s-front:0.4* image and expose it with a LoadBalancer Service.

Display the http://localhost:8080/files URL in your browser (it shows the names of all the files located in the */shared* folder of the container). No file should appear.

Update the Deployment so that the container sees the Secret object as files in its */shared* directory.

Refresh the http://localhost:8080/files page in your browser. The three entries from the Secret object should be shown (note that only the names of the files are displayed).

Display the http://localhost:8080/details URL in your browser. Note that there is no entry named *message*, *config* or *magicNumber*.

Update the Deployment so that the container sees all of the entries from the Secret object as environment variables.

Refresh the http://localhost:8080/details page in your browser. The three entries from the Secret object should be shown.

Delete all resources created.

7.7 Exercise solution

- Create a file named *commonvalues-secret.yaml* with the following contents:

```
apiVersion: v1
kind: Secret
metadata:
  name: commonvalues-secret
stringData:
  message: "Hello secret world"
  config: "Hidden"
  magicNumber: "0"
```

- Create a file named *front-deployment1.yaml* with the following contents:

```
apiVersion: apps/v1beta1
kind: Deployment
metadata:
  name: front
spec:
  template:
    metadata:
      labels:
        app: front
      spec:
```

```
containers:
- name: front
  image: learnbook/k8s-front:0.4
```

- Create a file named *front-service.yaml* with the following contents:

```
apiVersion: v1
kind: Service
metadata:
  name: front
spec:
  type: LoadBalancer
  ports:
  - port: 8080
    targetPort: 80
  selector:
    app: front
```

- Open a command-line in the folder where you created the above files.
- Run the following commands:

```
kubectl apply -f commonvalues-secret.yaml
kubectl apply -f front-deployment1.yaml
kubectl apply -f front-service.yaml
kubectl get secret
kubectl describe secret commonvalues-secret
```

You should get an output similar to the following one:

```
> kubectl apply -f commonvalues-secret.yaml

secret/commonvalues-secret created

> kubectl apply -f front-deployment1.yaml

deployment.apps/front created

> kubectl apply -f front-service.yaml

service/front created

> kubectl get secret

NAME                        TYPE       DATA   AGE
commonvalues-secret    Opaque      3      76s

> kubectl describe secret commonvalues-secret

Name:            commonvalues-secret
Namespace:       default
Labels:          <none>
Annotations:
```

```
Type:          Opaque

Data
====
config:        6 bytes
magicNumber:   1 bytes
message:       18 bytes
```

Point your browser to http://localhost:8080/files. No files are shown on the page.

- Create a file named *front-deployment2.yaml* by adding some entries to the *front-deployment1.yaml*. The *front-deployment2.yaml* should have the following contents:

```
apiVersion: apps/v1beta1
kind: Deployment
metadata:
  name: front
spec:
  template:
    metadata:
      labels:
        app: front
    spec:
      volumes:
        - name: shared
          secret:
            secretName: commonvalues-secret
```

```
containers:
- name: front
  image: learnbook/k8s-front:0.4
  volumeMounts:
    - mountPath: /shared
      name: shared
```

- In the command-line, run the following command:

```
kubectl apply -f front-deployment2.yaml
```

You should get an output similar to the following one:

```
> kubectl apply -f front-deployment2.yaml

deployment.apps/front configured
```

Refresh the http://localhost:8080/files page in your browser. Your browser should display a page listing the *config*, *magicNumber* and *message* files.

Point your browser to http://localhost:8080/details. No entry named *message*, *config* or *magicNumber* is displayed on the page.

- Create a file named *front-deployment4.yaml* by adding some entries to the *front-deployment1.yaml*. The *front-deployment4.yaml* should have the following contents:

```
apiVersion: apps/v1beta1
kind: Deployment
metadata:
  name: front
spec:
  template:
    metadata:
      labels:
        app: front
    spec:
      containers:
      - name: front
        image: learnbook/k8s-front:0.4
        envFrom:
          - secretRef:
              name: commonvalues-secret
```

- In the command-line, run the following command:

```
kubectl apply -f front-deployment4.yaml
```

You should get an output similar to the following one:

```
> kubectl apply -f front-deployment4.yaml

deployment.apps/front configured
```

Refresh the http://localhost:8080/details page in your browser. You should now see the *message*, *config* and *magicNumber* entries on the page.

- Run the following command:

```
kubectl delete -f .
```

8. Updating and scaling

8.1 Horizontal scaling

Horizontal scaling is a technique that allows an application to handle more concurrent requests, and is also called *scaling out*. When you run a server application on a machine (or a Pod for that matter), it can only handle a certain number of concurrent requests since each request requires some RAM and CPU resources.

For instance, your application may be able to handle 100 requests per second. If you want to handle more requests, you can duplicate the application on separate servers so that it handles more requests. Say we want to handle 300 requests per second, we can run 3 instances of our application.

On a traditional, server-hosted application, horizontal scaling requires some effort. The machine and its application need to be duplicated, and a load balancer application needs to be used in front of the three replicas so that incoming requests are served evenly by the three replicas. Good news: Kubernetes makes this task extremely easy. All you have to do is set a *replicas* property on the Deployment's definition:

```
apiVersion: apps/v1beta1
kind: Deployment
metadata:
  name: my-front
spec:
  replicas: 3
  template:
    metadata:
      labels:
        app: front
    spec:
      containers:
      - name: my-front
        image: my-wordpress
```

This definition states that three Pods are to be created. Kubernetes will ensure that three Pods are in a running state at all times, creating missing Pods or replacing failing ones as needed.

What about the load balancer that routes users to the three Pods? You already have it, and you don't need to modify it. At some point, in order to publicly expose even just a single Pod you created a LoadBalancer type Service that looks like:

```
apiVersion: v1
kind: Service
metadata:
  name: my-front-service
spec:
  type: LoadBalancer
  ports:
  - port: 8080
    targetPort: 80
  selector:
    app: front
```

Since that Service routes requests to any Pod that has a label *app* with the value *front*, it will naturally route requests to any of the three deployed Pods.

We already presented the ReplicaSet type and you may have wondered why this type exists between a Deployment and a Pod, as in the following image. The main difference between a ReplicaSet and a Deployment is that the ReplicaSet is responsible for running a specific number of replicas for a particular Pod (same specs for all the Pods), while the Deployment makes sure that the necessary ReplicaSet is created when you run the *kubectl apply* command. In case the *spec* part of a Deployment changes, a new ReplicaSet is created and the existing one is bound to be deleted.

The schema we saw for a ReplicaSet was the following:

This was when the Deployment didn't specify a *replica* count, so just one Pod was needed. Once we add the *replicas: 3* value to the Deployment, the ReplicaSet creates two additional Pods and makes sure to keep three Pods in a running state:

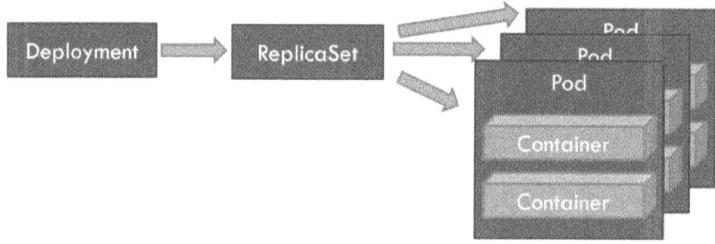

8.2 Automatic horizontal scaling

Scaling out was a difficult task but Kubernetes makes it easy. But we IT people always want more, so when some task becomes easy we look for more challenges. To be honest, the market is also asking for innovation so we also go the market way. How can we make horizontal scaling more challenging, then?

Consider this: it's fine to be able to set the number

of Pods that handle incoming requests, but how would you set that number? In case it is too low, the Pods won't be able to handle peaks in usage; in case it is too high, there will be too many Pods sitting around not doing much, which means they are consuming CPU and memory resources for nothing.

What would be great would be to dynamically change the number of Pods in order to meet the actual demand: when there are peaks of use, create more Pods, and when the application faces lower use, destroy useless Pods so that they free up resources.

Actually, this can be done by a simple Kubernetes object:

```
apiVersion: autoscaling/v1
kind: HorizontalPodAutoscaler
metadata:
  name: captureorder
spec:
  scaleTargetRef:
    apiVersion: apps/v1
    kind: Deployment
    name: front
  minReplicas: 4
  maxReplicas: 10
  targetCPUUtilizationPercentage: 70
```

That HorizontalPodAutoscaler monitors the CPU used by the available Pods, and compares it to the limits set by the Pod's cpu requests. In case the Pods use less than the target percentage, some Pods are destroyed. On the

contrary, when the Pods use more than the target percentage, new Pods are created until the target percentage is reached. Of course, the created number of Pods
will not exceed the *maxReplicas* stated in the definition,
and will not drop under the *minReplicas* number.

In the above example the automatic scaling is done
based on CPU usage but you can also use a target
memory usage.

In short, thanks to an HorizontalPodAutoscaler you can
define an application that will consume resources according to its actual usage, leaving room for other applications when it is under low use.

8.3 Update strategies

When you modify the template part of a Deployment,
existing Pods are no longer up to date, and need to
be replaced by Pods created using the new template.
As soon as you *kubectl apply* the modified Deployment,
Kubernetes handles this task for you. How exactly? Let's
see.

Since a ReplicaSet makes sure Pods of a given version
are running, once the version changes Kubernetes simply creates a new ReplicaSet. The older ReplicaSet will
delete the Pods it manages while the new one will create
Pods. The order in which those deletions and creations
take place is determined by the *stragegy* property of a
Deployment.

Recreate

When you set the strategy to *Recreate*, all of the older Pods are stopped first. Once they are no longer running, new Pods are started.

```
apiVersion: apps/v1beta1
kind: Deployment
metadata:
  name: my-front
spec:
  strategy:
    type: Recreate
  replicas: 3
  template:
    metadata:
      labels:
        app: front
    spec:
      containers:
      - name: my-front
        image: my-wordpress
```

The following sequence illustrates what happens when you *kubectl apply* changes to a Deployment's template with a recreate strategy.

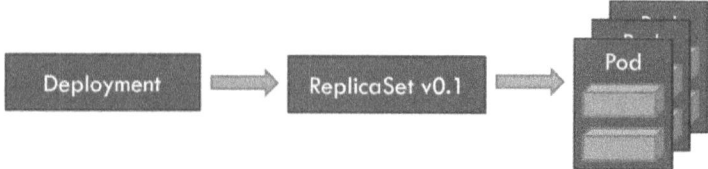

State before the Deployment change

Pods are stopped, then the ReplicaSet is deleted

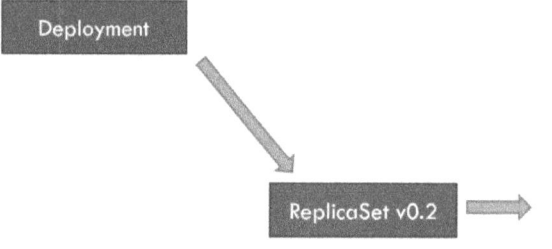

A new ReplicaSet is created

The new ReplicaSet creates Pods with the new template

A *Recreate* update strategy means that there will be no more Pods running at any given moment than the *replicas* count you set, so the update doesn't consume more resources than the running application. But it also means there will be a point at which no Pod is available, which means a service outage for your application. It's up to you to decide whether this is fine. In case it's not, the *RollingUpdate* strategy should look appealing to you.

Rolling update

Instead of stopping all existing Pods first and then create the new ones, there is a smoother approach that Kubernetes offers by default. All you have to do is specify a *RollingUpdate* value for the *strategy* type:

```
apiVersion: apps/v1beta1
kind: Deployment
metadata:
  name: my-front
spec:
  strategy:
    type: RollingUpdate
  replicas: 3
  template:
    metadata:
      labels:
        app: front
    spec:
      containers:
```

```
- name: my-front
  image: my-wordpress
```

In fact, *RollingUpdate* is the default value, so when we didn't specify any strategy type up to now, we had a rolling update strategy. That means you get a fine grained, high-availability and intelligent update at no cost with Kubernetes. Did I tell you that Kubernetes developers are lucky? Sure, it takes some knowledge to get up and running, but once you reach this point in the book you get fantastic powers that enable you to easily do what was very tedious. But let me detail how a rolling update takes place.

During a rolling update, Pods are replaced by batches of 25% (this is a default value that can be changed). A first batch of 25% (1 Pod when 3 are running, 2 Pods when 8 are running) of Pods are created using the new template. Kubernetes waits for the new Pods to be running, then stops the same quantity of old Pods. Once the old Pods are stopped, it repeats the process with another batch of 25% of the old Pods that are replaced by new Pods. That process is repeated until all the old Pods are replaced with new ones.

The rolling update process is even better: when the batch of 25% of new Pods is created, the Pods may fail; in case the new Pods can't reach a running state, the rolling update process stops and the old Pods are kept. This means that the application keeps running in case the new Pods are buggy; it is simply served by the old Pods while you can sort out and solve the problem with the new template and *kubectl apply* again.

In short, the rolling update process ensures that your application is always running even in case of a problem with the new version, and that few resources are used during the update process.

The following sequence illustrates what happens when you *kubectl apply* changes to a Deployment's template with a rolling update strategy.

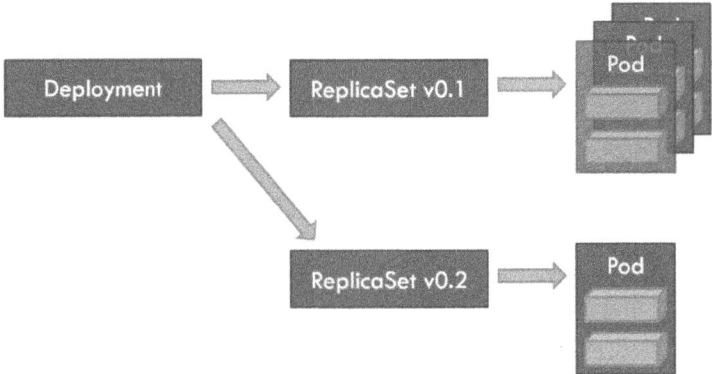

25% new Pods are created using the new template

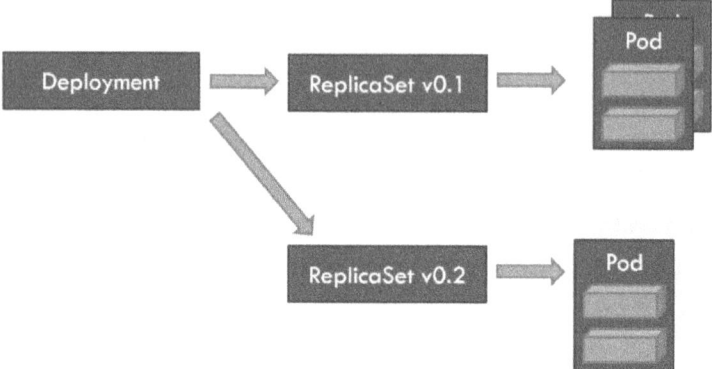

25% old Pods are deleted once the new ones are running

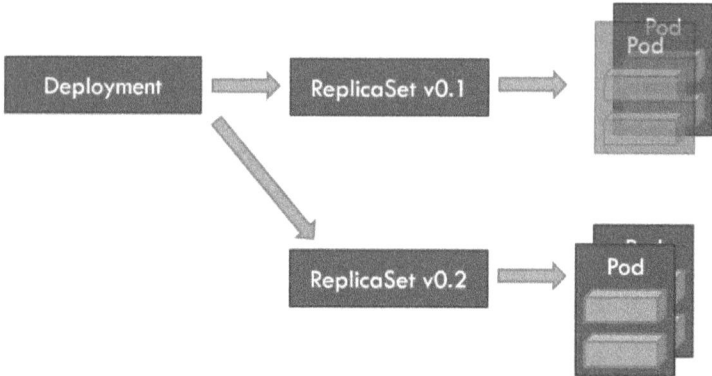

The process repeats with 25% of the Pods

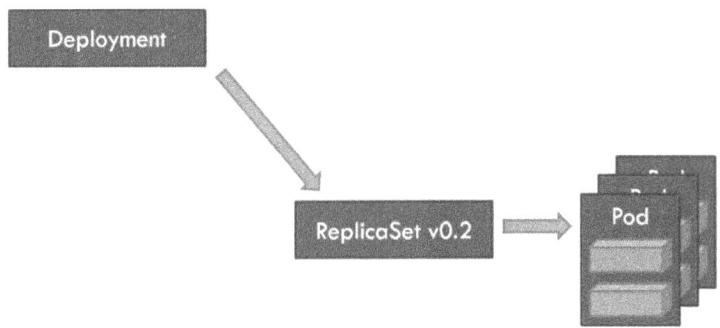

The old ReplicaSet is deleted

Rolling update parameters

In case you have advanced needs and all of this nifty rolling update isn't enough for you, it's possible to modify its behavior using some parameters:

```
apiVersion: apps/v1beta1
kind: Deployment
metadata:
  name: mon-front
spec:
  strategy:
    type: RollingUpdate
    rollingUpdate:
      maxSurge: 25%
      maxUnavailable: 25%
  replicas: 3
  template:
    spec:
      containers:
```

```
- name: mon-front
  image: mon-wordpress
```

The *maxSurge* and *maxUnavailable* parameters specify the batch size, that is, how many extra Pods may be created or left unavailable during an update. You can provide a number or a percentage. In the case of a percentage, it is relative to the *replicas* parameter.

Blue/green, canary and rainbow

The *rolling update* or *recreate* strategies should be fine for most needs, but if you are running an application that has a very high number of users you may want to go with more subtle update types. For all of those types you need to add some logic to your update process, and it is mostly done by tweaking the selector of the Service that route to your Pods.

During a blue/green update, a new version (blue) is created while users are routed to the old (green) version. The new version is tested, and once declared ready (green) it completely replaces the old one which in turn is deleted. You can do this by simply adding an extra blue/green label to your Pods and have two Services: one public for the green Pods, one private for the blue Pods.

A canary update tries to mimic the canary in a coal mine: as long as the bird was fine the miners knew they weren't facing the dangerous gaz. With a canary update, you instrument the application and route a little percentage of users to a new version while monitoring your metrics. If the metrics show problems, you decrease the percentage, and if the metrics are fine you increase the percentage. This can be achieved by matching the Service selector on some of the new Pods.

In extreme cases, you simply cannot stop an older version as long as it being used, but still want to publish a new version side-by-side. It's called a rainbow update since you will end up with different side-by-side versions of your application. This can be the case with microservices that introduce breaking changes. Using Namespaces you can quite easily deploy different versions of your application side-by-side, monitor the usage of each and kill the ones that aren't used anymore.

9. Sharing a cluster

9.1 Namespaces

Namespaces provide you with a way to isolate objects from one another inside a Kubernetes cluster. They allow for separation of object names, network names for Services, resource quotas and authorizations (RBAC).

Namespaces are a handy way to isolate teams inside a cluster: an object is scoped to its Namespace which avoids that a team modifies another team's object that has the same name.

A Kubernetes cluster starts with two Namespaces and you can add your own. The two default Namespaces are:

- *default* for objects that weren't assigned a Namespace.
- *kube-system* for objects that provide Kubernetes functionality.

You declare a Namespace like you would declare other Kubernetes objects:

```
apiVersion: v1
kind: Namespace
metadata:
  name: prod
```

Once a Namespace exists in your cluster, you can add the --namespace switch to the kubectl commands we already saw. For instance, the following command creates or updates in a namespace named *team1* the objects described in the *dep.yaml* file:

```
kubectl apply -f dep.yaml --namespace team1
```

Suppose that the *dep.yaml* file describes a Deployment named *front*. If you run the above command, the *front* Deployment and its Pods will be scoped to the *team1* namespace so you can run the same command in another *team2* namespace and get another "isolated" *front* deployment in the *team2* namespace:

```
kubectl apply -f dep.yaml --namespace team2
```

The same goes when you query Kubernetes resources. For instance, the following command returns Pods that belong to the *team1* namespace:

```
kubectl get pods --namespace team1
```

> When you run the same command without the --namespace switch you don't get the objects from all namespaces: you only get objects from the namespace named *default*. In case you want to list the Pods from all namespaces, use the --all-namespaces switch on the *kubectl get* command.

Since you're likely to work inside the same Namespace from day to day, you don't want to be adding the --namespace switch to each of your commands. Simply run the following command, and the current context will be set to work inside the *team1* Namespace by default:

```
kubectl config set-context --current --namespace=team1
```

From now on your commands will take place on objects inside the *team1* Namespace. Since the Namespace is associated with the kubectl context, it will be remembered when you switch to another context and back to the ones for which you set the context. In short: a kubectl context points to a cluster, a user **and a Namespace**.

We saw earlier that Services can be addressed using their names from inside the cluster, so a Service named *front* can be accessed over the http://front URL. Such DNS functionality is offered by the CoreDNS component. Better yet: a Service has two domain names: one that includes its Namespace and one that doesn't. For instance, the *front* Service has both domain names:

- *front.team1*
- *front*

The *front* domain name resolves to the Namespace from which a requests originates. So if a Pod from the *team2* Namespace queries the http://front URL it actually sees only a *front* Service from the *team2* Namespace. Should it need to address the Service from the *team1* Namespace, it could use the http://front.team1 URL. This name resolution again offers isolation between Namespaces: it avoids name conflicts while still allowing cross-Namespace communication.

Cluster administrators can use a *ResourceQuota* object. It allows for limiting the resources that can be used inside a Namespace. That way, objects from a Namespace cannot starve other Namespaces by taking up all of a cluster's resources. The following properties can be defined:

- limits.cpu: total of the CPU limits that can be requested by Pods;
- limits.memory: total of the memory limits that can be requested by Pods;
- requests.cpu: total of the CPU requests that can be made by Pods;
- requests.memory: total of the memory requests that can be made by Pods.

Note that some Kubernetes objects cannot be scoped to a Namespace and they live outside of Namespaces:

- Namespaces themselves;
- Nodes;
- PersistentVolumes.

9.2 RBAC

Up to now we've been doing fundamental changes inside our cluster simply using the *kubectl* command. This means that all you need in order to administer a cluster is a correct context. Now, imagine that some malicious user has access to such power: he would bring havoc to your cluster, get access to confidential information, or add malicious Pods in no time. You surely don't want this.

Apart from blocking external users, you also want to limit what specific users can do inside a Kubernetes cluster. For instance, in a pre-production cluster you may want to ensure that developers can only list Kubernetes objects but not change them, while the CI/CD engine would be the only one allowed to create or change objects. You may also want to ensure that only a specific user or system can create and read Secrets.

Such limitations can be defined using RBAC. You can link users (or service accounts) to specific permissions on the Kubernetes API.

Before you configure RBAC, you must ensure that your cluster has RBAC enabled. Since enabling the RBAC feature is a choice made when the cluster is created, you may not have information about whether that decision was made. In such a case, you may use the following command:

```
kubectl describe pod -n kube-system -l component=kube-a\
piserver
```

If RBAC is enabled on the cluster, you should see a mention of RBAC in the authorization mode:

```
--proxy-client-cert-file=/run/config/pki/front-p
--kubelet-preferred-address-types=InternalIP,Ext
--requestheader-extra-headers-prefix=X-Remote-Ex
--authorization-mode=Node,RBAC
--etcd-servers-https://127.0.0.1:2379
--etcd-cafile=/run/config/pki/etcd/ca.crt
--etcd-certfile=/run/config/pki/apiserver-etcd-c
--etcd-keyfile=/run/config/pki/apiserver-etcd-cl
State:           Running
```

Just like many authorization systems, RBAC doesn't directly link users to permissions. Instead, it links permissions to Roles, and users are assigned to Roles. This allows for easily adding and removing users as your team changes, and for reconfiguring rights for a group in a snap. In short, Roles are user groups.

There are two types of roles:

- Role: defines authorizations that are scoped to a namespace;
- ClusterRole: defines authorizations that are valid across the whole cluster.

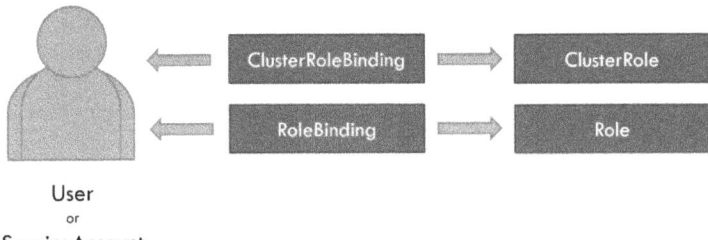

User
or
ServiceAccount

A *RoleBinding* connects one User (or ServiceAccount) to a Role. Symmetrically, a *ClusterRoleBinding* connects one User (or ServiceAccount) to a ClusterRole.

In order for a RBAC-enabled cluster to function, some ClusterRoles are already defined, and bound to the User that you are using to connect from your *kubectl* command-line. Here are some of the ClusterRoles in my cluster:

```
> kubectl get clusterroles
```

```
NAME                                       AGE
admin                                      8d
cluster-admin                              8d
edit                                       8d
system:coredns                             8d
system:persistent-volume-provisioner       8d
view                                       8d
```

The list above was edited for brevity. You can see three ClusterRoles that are commonly used, and that you can assign to new users if you don't want to spend time creating your own roles. The *admin* and *cluster-admin* roles have extended permissions and should be granted with due care. You can examine the authorizations assigned to a role with the following command:

```
> kubectl describe clusterrole view
```

```
Name:        view
Labels:      kubernetes.io/bootstrapping=rbac...
             rbac.authorization.k8s.io/aggreg...
Annotations: rbac.authorization.kubernetes.io...
PolicyRule:
  Resources                     Verbs
  ---------                     -----
  configmaps                    [get list watch]
  persistentvolumeclaims        [get list watch]
  pods/log                      [get list watch]
  pods/status                   [get list watch]
  pods                          [get list watch]
```

That list was again edited for brevity. We can see that the *view* ClusterRole has the ability to list pods, so the *kubectl get logs* command would be granted for that role.

10. Helm

10.1 Using Helm

Helm is coined as "The package manager for Kubernetes":

Screenshot from the Helm web site

I wouldn't compare Helm to package managers like NPM or NuGet that also manage your packages' dependencies, but it sure means an easy path when you want to deploy complex applications to Kubernetes.

Practically speaking, it mainly allows to add extra power to the *kubectl apply* command: it enables the use of variables and even scripting inside YAML files, then those files are packed together. Helm packages are called *Charts*.

The easiest part in Helm is using an existing Chart, that is, installing an application in a Kubernetes cluster using a Helm chart. It is done in two steps:

1. add a Helm repository (the source for charts, just like a Registry for Docker Images);
2. install a chart using the following command:

```
helm install <name> --set version=1.0,key=value,... <ch\
art>
```

The `--set` switch allows you to override default values from the chart. When there are many values, you can instead provide them in a YAML file.

Let's take an example to illustrate this. Suppose I want to install Redis. Redis is a distributed cache, which means values are stored across different machines: a great example of something that can easily be distributed across different Pods on several Nodes.

From the Redis chart description[1] I can see that the number of slaves to create is set by the *cluster.slaveCount* variable. It has a default of 1 and I want to override it to 3 so that I have 4 Pods running my Redis cluster (1 master, 3 slaves).

---

[1] https://github.com/helm/charts/tree/master/stable/redis

```
> helm repo add stable https://kubernetes-charts.storag\
e.googleapis.com/

"stable" has been added to your repositories

> helm install mycache stable/redis --set cluster.slave\
Count=3

NAME: mycache
LAST DEPLOYED: Thu Jan 30 14:07:47 2020
NAMESPACE: default
STATUS: deployed
REVISION: 1
TEST SUITE: None
NOTES:
** Please be patient while the chart is being deployed \
**
Redis can be accessed via port 6379 on the following DN\
S names from within your cluster:


mycache-redis master.default.svc.cluster.local for read\
/write operations
mycache-redis-slave.default.svc.cluster.local for read-\
only operations


To get your password run:
...
```

The output has been shortened for brevity, but as you can see upon installation a chart provides some documentation based on the parameters you provided.

Let's list the Pods running in my cluster:

```
> kubectl get pods
```

```
NAME                       READY   STATUS    AGE
mycache-redis-master-0     1/1     Running   3m20s
mycache-redis-slave-0      1/1     Running   3m20s
mycache-redis-slave-1      1/1     Running   2m34s
mycache-redis-slave-2      1/1     Running   2m17s
```

Alright, I really have 4 Pods running Redis. Just that simple.

10.2 Creating Helm packages (charts)

We just saw how a well-made chart eases deployment of complex applications. Once you create a Kubernetes-ready application you will probably want to package it as a chart for an easier distribution. Mind you, it's quite an easy process.

A chart actually is a collection of files in a *.tar.gz package:

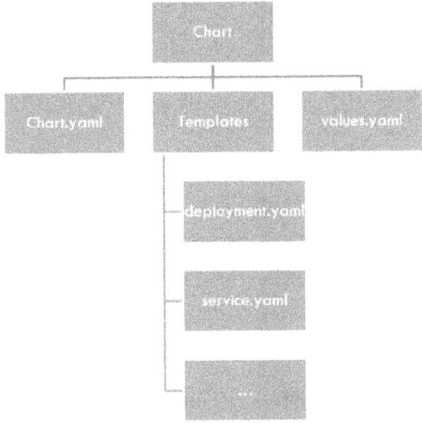

The files are:

- YAML files that describe Kubernetes objects just like the ones we saw up to now, but with the possibility to add scripting;
- A values.yaml file that defines the default values for variables used in your scripting;
- A NOTES.txt file that will render the help text when the chart is installed.

As mentioned, in the YAML file you can use YAML syntax, and you can add script blocks: for that matter, Go templates are used:

```
apiVersion: apps/v1beta1
kind: Deployment
metadata:
  name: back-{{ .Values.config }}
```

The above file defines a Deployment, and the name of that deployment will be generated by appending a *config* entry to the back- prefix. The actual value of the *config* entry is set in the *values.yaml* file but can be overridden using the --set switch or a YAML file upon install.

Instead of starting with a blank folder, you can scaffold a chart template with the following command:

```
helm create <name>
```

That simply creates a folder with enough starter files to have an actual chart. You then edit the files to suit your needs. Any YAML file you place in the *templates* directory will be part of the chart.

You then create the chart using the following commands (lint is just for verification purposes):

```
helm lint <name>
helm package <name> --debug
```

That creates an installable chart in a file named <name>-0.1.0.tgz (the version comes from the Chart.yaml file). Before you distribute your chart, you may want to check what it actually does. That can be done with the following command that will output the YAML that will be sent to the Kubernetes cluster instead of actually applying it to a cluster:

```
helm install --dry-run --debug <name>-0.1.0.tgz
```

You can now distribute your chart in one of two ways:

- distribute the *.tar.gz file;
- place the *.tar.gz file on a Helm repository (simple an HTTP file server hosting the *.tar.gz files).

When distributed as a file, the chart can be installed using the file name:

```
helm install <name> --set version=1.0,key=value,... <ch\
art>-0.1.0.tgz
```

When distributed using a repository, users will simply need to add your repository using the helm repo add command.

A word from the author

I sincerely hope you enjoyed reading this book as much as I liked writing it and that you quickly become proficient enough with deploying your applications over Kubernetes clusters.

If you would like to get in touch you can use:

- email: books@aweil.fr
- Facebook: https://facebook.com/learncollection
- Twitter: @epo

In case your project needs it, I'm also available for speaking, teaching, consulting and coding, all around the world.

If you liked this book, you probably saved a lot of time thanks to it. I'd be very grateful if you took some minutes of your precious time to leave a comment on the site where you purchased this book. Thanks a ton!

Image attributions

- Classic ship loading: public domain, from Wikimedia Commons[2]
- Container ship loading: public domain, Tvabutzku1234, from Wikimedia Commons[3].
- Freight train: public domain, G-Man March 2005, from Wikimedia Commons[4], originally uploaded to the English Wikipedia.

---

[2]https://commons.wikimedia.org/wiki/File:Korean-war-merchant-marine-load.jpg#file
[3]https://commons.wikimedia.org/wiki/File:Container_ship_Yorktown_Express_(2).jpg
[4]https://commons.wikimedia.org/wiki/File:WCML_freight_train.jpg

The Learn collection

This book is part of the *Learn collection*.

The *Learn collection* allows developers to self-teach new technologies in a matter of days.

Published books

- Learn ASP.NET Core MVC[5]
- Learn ASP.NET MVC[6]
- Learn Docker[7]
- Learn Kubernetes[8]
- Learn Meteor[9]
- Learn Microservices[10]
- Learn WPF MVVM[11]

To be published

- Learn Unit Testing

---

[5]https://leanpub.com/netcore
[6]https://leanpub.com/aspnetmvc
[7]https://leanpub.com/dock
[8]https://leanpub.com/kubernetes
[9]https://leanpub.com/learnmeteor
[10]https://leanpub.com/micro
[11]https://leanpub.com/learnwpf